Ideas A-Z:
Christmas

Phyllis Vos Wezeman
Anna L. Liechty
Judith Harris Chase

DEDICATION

To The David Peyton Family ... friends with whom we have celebrated many special seasons! P.V.W.

SPECIAL THANKS TO

Ron Liechty and Ken Wezeman
for technical and theological support!

IDEAS A-Z: CHRISTMAS
by Phyllis Vos Wezeman, Anna L. Liechty and Judith Harris Chase
Copyright ©2000 Educational Ministries, Inc.

Printed in the United States of America. All rights reserved. No portion of this book may be reproduced except for classroom use without the prior permission of the copyright owner.

ISBN 1-57438-043-5
Educational Ministries, Inc.
165 Plaza Dr.
Prescott, AZ 86303
800-221-0910

TABLE OF CONTENTS

INTRODUCTION	5
OVERVIEW	7
A: ANTIPHONS	11
B: BULLETIN BOARDS	13
C: COSTUMES	17
D: DOUGH	22
E: ENVIRONMENT	24
F: FIGURES	27
G: GREENS	33
H: HYMN STORY	35
I: INTERGENERATIONAL	37
J: JESSE TREE	46
K: KIDS	48
L: LIGHT	50
M: MUSIC	54
N: NURTURE	57
O: OVERHEAD	60

P: PUPPETS	66
Q: QUESTIONS	68
R: RIBBONS	70
S: SENSES	72
T: TABLEAUS	78
U: USE	80
V: VISUALS	82
W: WISE MEN	84
X: X-CHANGE	86
Y: YOUTH	88
Z: Z-A PEOPLE	90
RESOURCES	93

INTRODUCTION

Taking a look at the shelves in Christian bookstores, one can almost come to a conclusion that writers of religious education books have taken too literally God's command to "be fruitful and multiply." With the deluge of available materials, why on earth do we offer the Ideas A-Z series? There are many answers to this question.

First of all, Ideas A-Z provides an in-depth look at Scripture, both the people and the important themes. Using twenty-six different viewing points assures readers of thoughtful and thorough reflection on Biblical topics. Each perspective provides opportunities for experiencing the lesson on a variety of levels, allowing readers and participants to discover the story in a way appropriate to their stages in life and faith development.

Ideas A-Z also develops a unique format for delivering insights, information, and activities. The A-Z topics offer a balanced variety of methods and approaches for experiencing the Biblical story. For every letter of the alphabet there is a different theme and a different way of exploring that theme, like drama, games, music, puppetry or storytelling. Such experiential learning also takes into consideration the needs of all learning styles, or multiple intelligences.

Another aspect of the format is its flexibility. Each idea, A through Z, can be used alone or combined with other letters to develop a lesson plan, a worship experience, or an intergenerational activity. The ideas offered can simply be used to supplement existing curricula, or they can be referred to like a handbook. The format is user-friendly and open-ended, providing essential information, yet fostering creative applications.

From beginning students of the Bible to more advanced learners, Ideas A-Z can inspire and motivate participants to keep looking at the Scriptures in fresh ways and to keep applying the Bible's principles to their own lives.

So although the Christmas story has been told, re-told, written about, and re-written countless times, Ideas A-Z offers participants an opportunity to explore and experience the message anew — from beginning to end, from A to Z.

OVERVIEW

WHO?

First, the "Who" of Christmas is God: the God who made the universe, who was saddened to see creation fall, and who designed a plan for redemption through the birth, life, death, and resurrection of Jesus.

Next, the "Who" of Christmas is Jesus, Himself: God-in-flesh, who came to earth to bring hope, to show us the way and to be the Way. The challenge of Christmas is to appreciate the humanity of Jesus who was born as a baby in Bethlehem and to worship the divine Jesus who conquered death and sin for us.

The third "who" in the story is people like us, the ones for whom Christ was born. However, the victory of Christmas is only complete when the power of the story of Christmas, the Ever-Present-Spirit of God, is re-born again in each of our hearts to renew and resurrect God's creation.

WHAT?

Calendars help provide the structure for all aspects of our lives, and the church is no exception. Just like the secular calendar reminds us of Valentine hearts or Thanksgiving turkeys, the church calendar invites us to experience the festivals of faith. The church year coordinates the message of six basic seasons, with slight variations among the denominations. From Advent to Pentecost we experience the life and ministry of Jesus, and the empowering of His church to carry on the work God began in creation. Those stories become part of the rhythm of our lives — anticipated, celebrated, savored, and shared by all God's people. Rather than treasured fragments of disconnected text, the Bible becomes the woven fabric of a seamless garment, with each season flowing meaningfully to the next, completing the cycle, yet leading us to begin again the wonderful journey of faithful discipleship. To understand the focus and flavor of the church year, the following material provides an overview of basic background information for the season of Christmas, as well as the season that precedes it — Advent — and the season that follows it — Epiphany.

CHRISTMAS

Christmas is the twelve-day season from December 25th until January 6th. Carols are sung, the Christmas story read, and the birth of Jesus celebrated.

The color for Christmas is usually white.

ADVENT

Advent is the season of preparation for the coming of Christ, beginning four Sundays prior to Christmas. During Advent, the church prepares for the birth of Jesus as a babe in a manger in history and for the birth of Christ's presence in the hearts of faithful people. As well, Advent is a time to remember that we also wait for Christ's promised return to the world, called the "second coming." Scripture lessons focus on prophecy, especially Isaiah's foretelling of the Messiah and John the Baptist's announcements of the need for repentance and preparation for the One who is to come.

The color for Advent is usually purple, representing both the darkness of the world without Christ and the royal purple fit for a king. The color blue, for hope, has been employed during this season, too. If an Advent wreath is used, often purple candles are lit, one each week signifying that the light of Christ is coming closer. Traditionally, the third candle is pink to suggest joy. On Christmas Sunday, and/or Christmas Eve, a white Christ Candle is lit to announce the birth of Jesus, the Light of the World.

EPIPHANY

Epiphany is the season from January 6th until the beginning of Lent, although some churches observe a season of "ordinary time" between the Festival of the Epiphany and the Lenten season. Epiphany means literally "appearance" or "revelation." At this time, Christians celebrate the arrival of the "wise men from the East" at the manger of Bethlehem, signifying God's gift being made available to all people. Simultaneously, Epiphany is the date set for remembering Christ's baptism. Scripture readings focus on the story of the magi and the Gospel accounts of John's baptism of Jesus. The season of Epiphany is a time of celebrating new revelations of God's presence among us.

For the Festival of Epiphany the appropriate color is white, although gold is sometimes used as the color of the star and the gift brought the Christ child. Those churches who designate part of this season as Ordinary Time often use green as the interim color prior to Lent.

WHEN?

TIME LINE

A time line provides a way to put the events of history in order — to actually visualize what happened at what point in time. Because the Christian world uses the birth of Jesus to divide and date history, abbreviations in a time line often include B.C., B.C.E, and A.D. B.C. stands for before Christ, B.C.E. refers to before the common era or before the

Christian era, and A.D., the Latin words Anno Domini, mean "in the year of our Lord." The letter c., an abbreviation for circa, before a date means around or about that year. It is important to note that dates vary depending on the reference material used to compile a time line. Use the time line provided as a guide for putting Biblical events into perspective, but refer to additional resources to supplement the information.

TIME LINE

Undated - Creation
Undated - Adam and Eve; Sin; Cain and Abel
Undated - Noah; Flood
Undated - Tower of Babel
2100 B.C. - Abraham
2066 B.C. - Abraham and Isaac
2006 B.C. - Jacob and Esau
1900 B.C. - Joseph in Egypt
1700 B.C. - 1250 B.C. - Hebrews in Egypt
1526 B.C. - Moses born
1450 B.C. - Exodus; Moses and the Law
1399 B.C.- Joshua; Promised Land
1375 B.C. - Judges begin to rule Israel
1209 B.C. - Deborah
1162 B.C. - Gideon
1105 B.C. - Samuel born
1070 B.C. - Samson
1050 B.C.- Saul becomes Israel's first king
1000-961 B.C. - David king
970 B.C.- Solomon king
959 B.C. - Temple in Jerusalem completed
930 B.C.- Kingdom of Israel divides
875 B.C.- Elijah and prophets
793 B.C.- Jonah
740 B.C. - Isaiah
605 B.C. - Daniel
586 B.C. - Jerusalem/Temple destroyed
537 B.C. - First Jewish exiles return from captivity
516 B.C. - New Temple completed in Jerusalem
479 B.C. - Mordecai, Esther & Haman
445 B.C. - Nehemiah builds Jerusalem wall
333 B.C. - Judea made part of Greek empire
63 B.C. - Rome occupies Judea
40-4 B.C. - Herod the Great king of Judea
7-4 B.C. - Jesus born
26/27 A.D. - John the Baptist preaching
26/27 A.D. - Jesus baptized
30 A.D. - Crucifixion
30 A.D. - Pentecost
35 A.D. - Paul converted
40 A.D. - James martyred
45 A.D. - Paul's journeys begin
45-90 A.D. - Letters to Christians
67 A.D. - Paul martyred
70 A.D. - Romans destroy Jerusalem
150 A.D. - All books of New Testament completed

WHERE?
MAP

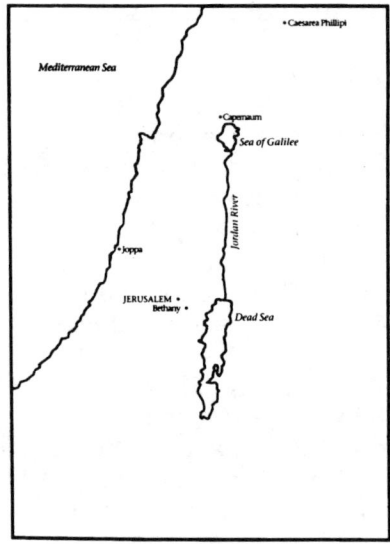

WHERE?

SCRIPTURE
Scripture passages related to the story of Jesus' birth and the events that preceded and followed it include:
Matthew 1:1 & 2;
Luke 1 & 2;
John 1:1-14.

Numerous Old Testament references anticipate the coming of the Messiah, and many New Testament verses confirm Christ as the Savior of the world.

WHY?

Why do we tell the Christmas Story every year? Once we hear it, isn't that enough? The details don't change: shepherds, angels, mother, baby, magi, star. Who wouldn't understand that simple drama in one reading?

Yet, somehow, we are captured each year. We hear some part of the story in a new way, or at a new depth because WE change. Each reading of the Christmas Story invites us to recognize anew that we are the one who needs the Savior, we are the one whom "God so loved."

The test of a good story is that it can be read over and over and still retain its freshness, still retain its power to move and change us. Such a story is the Christmas Story. We study God's simple plan to change the world, and we discover its power for our own lives.

A: ANTIPHONS

PURPOSE

To learn the history and meaning of "Antiphons" and to write an original "antiphon" in preparation for Christmas.

PREPARATION

- Paper
- Pencils or pens
- Church History books
- Hymnals
- Denominational Books of Worship

PROCEDURE

An "Antiphon" is a type of hymn or psalm that is meant to be sung responsively, in alternating parts. In the early history of the church, monks and other religious persons sang antiphons as morning and evening prayers, and sang them as well throughout the day in what was called the "Liturgy of the Hours." One of the most familiar antiphonal hymns still sung today is "O Come, O Come, Emmanuel." This Advent hymn is sung as a prayer to Christ to return to earth. There were many songs of this type in the Middle Ages; so many that they are usually grouped as the "O Antiphons," and many are still related to the Christmas season.

Traditionally, the "O Antiphon" begins with a name for God or Jesus, and is a prayerful plea for divine presence. Many names for God are used in the antiphons. Some names address God, for example: "O Wisdom," "O Creator, "O Rock of My Salvation." Some address Jesus: "O Sacred Lord," "O Light, "O Dayspring." Any name may be chosen that characterizes a quality of the Divine Trinity. After naming God, the antiphon often includes a descriptive phrase that further captures the characteristics suggested by the name for God. Also the antiphon usually includes a direct request of God, beginning with the word "Come." Refer to books of church history, books of Christmas devotions and prayers, hymnals, or denominational books of worship for examples.

Today Christians still value the "O Antiphons." Faithful people still call to God in longing and in love. The "O Antiphons" can be used as bedtime prayers, table graces, family devotions, classroom activities, or candle-lighting sentences in preparation for Christmas. As a part of Christmas preparation and celebration, write some "O Antiphons" to use this season. Include a name for God and a phrase that captures an attribute of God or that relates to the chosen name. Next develop a request of God that begins with the word "Come." For example:

Name of God

O Source of Peace,

Attribute of God

Whose Presence calms our restless hearts,

Request of God

Come to our home this Christmas
As we open our lives to Your gift of Jesus.

Use original "O Antiphons" as messages for packages and cards, as table place cards, or as spoken prayers. Consider reading the "O Antiphons" aloud antiphonally, dividing phrases between two individuals or groups.

B: BULLETIN BOARDS

PURPOSE

To create bulletin boards on Christmas themes.

PREPARATION

- ❏ Bulletin board(s)
- ❏ Background cloth or paper
- ❏ Scissors
- ❏ Glue, pins, stapler and staples, tape
- ❏ Letter patterns
- ❏ Materials to create the bulletin board

PROCEDURE

Bulletin boards provide an excellent way to reinforce a seasonal theme and to decorate wall space. Displays can be simple with handmade or purchased components. Try cooperative or interactive arrangements which allow for many designers to contribute to the final results.

Simplify the preparation of bulletin board backgrounds by using large rolls of paper such as gift wrap, wallpaper or butcher paper. Cover framed areas quickly with paper tablecloths, fabric or posterboard.

Keep captions short in order to get the attention of viewers and to avoid cutting dozens of letters. Investigate craft shops, teaching materials stores or office supply centers for die-cut and pin-back letters. Check with local schools or resource centers for an Ellison machine, which cuts several letters at once.

Add three dimensional items for special interest and place a border around the edge to give a finished look.

Consider a rotating schedule for bulletin board responsibility or designate one person to coordinate displays. Plan to change designs about once a month! A "rule of thumb" suggests that after viewing a bulletin board on five or six different occasions, people no longer notice it.

Try any or all of these five bulletin board suggestions to help people experience the Christmas message through sight, smell, sound, taste and touch.

SIGHT: INSPIRATIONAL BULLETIN BOARD

Make use of beautiful Christmas cards, pictures from curriculum packets or old issues of magazines for a simple and inspirational bulletin board. Reproductions of paintings by famous artists are excellent for a religious holiday theme.

Cover the background with velvet fabric for a look of elegance. Mount larger pictures on gold paper lace or frame the pictures with wide gold ribbon. Pictures from greeting cards can be mounted on gold lace doilies to resemble ornaments or medallions. Allow ample space for a caption, Scripture reference and border. Do not place pictures too close together so the beauty of each one can be appreciated separately.

Choose a caption that relates to the theme of the pictures featured. Write "See His Star" if most of the illustrations include stars, Bethlehem and Wise Men; "Behold, I bring you good news" would be appropriate for pictures of the Holy Family, angels and shepherds. Frame the display with wide gold ribbon.

SMELL: GRAFFITI BOARD

Our sense of smell is very closely connected to our ability to remember. Think of how many Christmas memories are associated with a particular scent: pine, citrus, peppermint, spices, fresh baked goods, special holiday foods and bayberry candles.

Cover a bulletin board with white paper. Arrange a garland of real or artificial evergreens around the frame. Real greens will smell great, but might shed. Attach small wrapped peppermint candies or candy canes for color as well as for a sweet scent.

Cut or purchase three or four inch red letters for the caption: "Christmas smells like..." Use a long red ribbon to tie on a red marking pen. Invite everyone to write Christmas "smell" memories on this graffiti board. Top off the board with a big red bow.

SOUND: "MAKE A JOYFUL NOISE UNTO THE LORD"

Cover a bulletin board with red paper or fabric. Form artificial evergreens into a wreath, then fasten securely to the center portion of the board. Decorate the evergreens with musical instrument ornaments. Instruments are available in several sizes wherever Christmas decorations are sold.

Use the Scripture phrase from Psalm 100: "Make a Joyful Noise Unto The Lord..." Position the caption in the center of the wreath, directly on the red paper or on a separate sheet of paper. Use a marker with a wide tip, a calligraphy pen or small cut out letters. Cut small musical notes from construction paper for a border or to scatter in the open areas.

This bulletin board design could be a perfect backdrop for announcements of church musical events or community concerts. Make the wreath smaller and staple the announcements around the edges.

TASTE: RECIPE EXCHANGE

Cover the bulletin board with a red and white checkered tablecloth or one with a Christmas design. In the center of the cover, fasten a table setting: large white, red or green paper plate; foam or paper cup; plastic knife, spoon and fork; holiday napkin. Use long dressmaker pins or corsage pins to attach items that cannot be stapled.

Print or cut letters for "Holiday Favorites" or "A Taste of Christmas" with a subtitle: "Recipe Exchange." Place a table for supplies under the bulletin board. Provide baskets of index cards, pens, pencils and tacks. Invite church members to write out a "family favorite" recipe, sign their names and add to the display. When the bulletin board fills up with a variety of recipes, gather up the cards and have photocopies made. Add the copies to the supply table.

For a true "Taste of Christmas," plan to have samples of the foods as well as recipes available at a special holiday event!

TOUCH: CHRISTMAS STORY IN TEXTURE

So many times we are told, "Don't touch!" Experiment with a tactile display that encourages everyone to "Please Touch!" Cover the bulletin board with light or dark blue paper and in the center staple a traditional picture with the Holy Family, angels, kings and shepherds.

Create a random collage or "crazy quilt" of textures surrounding the picture. Choose textures that relate to the Christmas story: feathers for angels; soft blanket for the Baby Jesus; rough fabric for the clothing of Joseph and the shepherds; fleece or wool for the sheep; straw or hay and wood slats for the crib; satins, brocades, velvets and jewels for the kings.

If children will be working on this display, read the Christmas story and ask them to think of different types of materials. Each person may contribute a fabric or textured item for the display. Use duct tape or staples to fasten materials so that there are no sharp points to injure exploring fingers!

The collage will have a balanced look if materials, colors and textures are repeated across the board. Add the words, "Please Touch!" Place the caption under the bulletin board frame or write the words on a band of wide ribbon and fasten it diagonally across one corner.

C: COSTUMES

PURPOSE

To discover numerous ways to create costumes for use in holiday pageants and programs.

PREPARATION

❑ Supplies vary with project.

PROCEDURE

Bring holiday pageants and programs to life with costuming. Costumes may be as elaborate or as simple as budget and time allow. Keep in mind that the main purpose of dramatic presentations is to "tell the story;" costumes are intended to enhance the message. Designing and creating appropriate clothing can be an important activity that adds to the educational value of dramatic productions. In order to elevate costuming to a level beyond bathrobes and sheets, gather information from books about historical costumes or search for clothing illustrations in biblical reference materials and story books. Occasionally, major companies, such as Mc Calls and Simplicity include instructions for biblical garments in seasonal pattern books. If such examples are not available, modify patterns for caftans, robes, capes, vests, tunics or other simple clothing.

Basic garments worn by Hebrews involved very little structure. Men, women and children wore a basic tunic. It was worn next to the skin and went either to the knees or ankles. The tunic for men was belted with a band of fabric or leather known as the girdle. The cloak or mantle, called *aba* in Hebrew, was made of a heavier fiber, usually wool, and was worn over the tunic. It served as protection from the rain or cold and doubled as a covering at night. It typically had short sleeves or slits for armholes and was long enough to extend below the knees. The head covering for men was either a turban or a head cloth. To form a turban, a long strip of heavy fabric was wrapped around the head several times and the ends were tucked in the folds to secure. The head cloth, *kaffiyeh*, was a large square of material held in place by a coil of fabric or rope. Both of the headdresses were needed as protection from sun and sand.

Women wore tunics, as well, but for them it was an undergarment. Over the tunic they wore a garment similar in shape, but of heavier fabric that became the dress. For warmth, a cloak or mantle was added. Women's clothing was longer than men's and was usually decorated with needlework. They wore a sash of cloth to hold the garments close to the body. On their heads, women wore a tight-fitting cap adorned with coins, declaring the family's wealth. A long veil was worn over the cap to cover the head and most of the face when going out in public.

Children wore the same basic tunic, but it was usually shorter and unbelted to allow for freer movement. In most cases, neutral-colored materials were used.

Costumes for the Wise men may require some research to learn about Oriental, Persian or African clothing styles. All can have the tunic as a foundation with capes, panels or draping added. Interesting headgear will add drama to the outfits.

Most of the costumes can be made with very little sewing using inexpensive materials or ready-made clothing. Begin searching for Christmas pageant props and materials for garments during summer garage sales. Check thrift shops and rummage sales during the year for possible fabrics and ready-made items which can be adapted. Be sure to ask members of the congregation to check fabric supplies and closets! Launder the materials, then store them in trunks or boxes according to "character." When the time comes to fashion angels, kings, and so forth, materials needed will be in one place.

Allow adequate time to research clothing styles, to gather materials, and to create costumes. Enlist the help of people familiar with stage production, sewing, fashion, and patterns. Find volunteers to scour garage sales and thrift shops for costuming treasures. Designate a photographer and record keeper. Assemble a costume "team" so no one person has to do all of the work. With all of the arrangements for the dramatic presentation, remember — and remind others — that the main purpose of all of the preparation is to "tell the story."

Consider the following items for creating costumes:

YARD GOODS AND REMNANTS

Select medium to heavy weight fabric in stripes, plain colors and rougher textures for Joseph, shepherds, and townspeople; brocade, satin and velvet for kings; lighter weight fabrics for Mary and the angels; gold lame for headpieces or halos.

SHEETS

Use striped or plain sheets for tunics and head coverings.

BLANKETS AND BEDSPREADS

Choose any weight blankets or spreads for cloaks or mantles; heavier weight for shepherds; luxurious quilted spreads for kings.

CURTAINS AND DRAPERIES

Look for various textures for mantles, cloaks, tunics and head coverings; filmy or lacy fabric is suitable for angels and Mary. Drapery linings may be used, as well.

TABLE LINENS

Choose striped linens or tablecloths with border designs for tunics or head coverings. Table runners can be used as sashes or decorative panels.

BATHROOM CARPET

Simulate fleece or sheepskin for shepherds. Fashion vests of white, beige, tan or gray easy-to-cut carpet or small rugs.

FAKE FUR AND FLEECE

Find remnants or coat linings for shepherds. A zip-out lining that looks like fur or fleece is ready to use ... cut off any sleeve linings.

TRIMS

Look for jewel-like buttons, braid, fringe or fancy appliques for adorning garments and headpieces of kings.

NECKTIES AND SCARVES

Make sashes or belts with neckties or by twisting scarves into a narrow band; fashion headdress from scarves or ties.

BATHROBES, CAFTANS OR LONG TEE SHIRTS

Use robes of velour, satin or velvet for the kings outer garment; caftans or long tees for tunics or basic costume.

SKIRTS, VESTS, BLOUSES

Consider ready-made clothes for parts of costumes: wooly or textured vests for shepherds, long tapestry vests for kings; "dressy" tops or blouses in jewel tones for kings; skirts with elastic in the waist as a basic garment for kings. Pull a longer skirt up under the arms and layer a shorter skirt over the person's shoulders to form the top or cape.

COAT LININGS

Cut out or unzip coat linings for parts of costumes; choose appropriate lining for different characters.

FORMALS AND BRIDAL GOWNS

Use parts of gowns for elegant fabrics and trims; bridal gown material might work for angel garments or wings.

SANDALS OR SLIPPERS

Choose leather or canvas thongs or sandals for most participants; "glitzy" clogs, sandals or slippers would be great for kings.

LEATHER PURSES, BELTS, LEATHER STRAPS

Find an old purse to fashion a bag or pouch for shepherds or travelers; look for leather belts and straps for rustic costumes.

FELT OR CLOTH HATS

Choose turban-style hats or use a cloth or felt hat as a base for the turban-like "crowns" most likely worn by "visitors from the East." Use elegant fabrics and embellish with trims and "jewels."

ROPE, HEAVY YARN OR DRAPERY CORDS

Adjust garments to fit a range of sizes by sashing and "blousing" fabric to shorten or lengthen. Crisscross gold or satin cord across the bodice of angel costumes for decoration or to help hold wings.

COSTUME JEWELRY OR FAUX JEWELS

Recycle broken pins, single earrings, decorative buttons, medallions and large beads; buy large faux jewels or bicycle reflectors for "flash!"

JEWELRY CHEST OR HINGED BOX

Paint gold or trim with jewels.

URNS, BOTTLES WITH STOPPERS, VASES

Paint gold or cover with florists' foil; add jewels.

WOODEN POLES OR RODS

Use large wooden poles for shepherds crooks — clothesline poles, closet rods, saplings — or cut staff from plywood or heavy cardboard.

MISCELLANEOUS NOTIONS

Safety pins for costume adjustments; sewing supplies; duct tape for alterations and repair; scissors; stiff interfacing for crowns, halos or wings; boxes for storing costumes and accessories.

CAMERA, FILM AND PHOTO ALBUM

Take photos of each costume and write down helpful details; keep information in an album with costumes. If the costume has several parts, sketch or photograph its construction step-by-step.

D: DOUGH

PURPOSE

To develop activities using bread to nurture the family of faith.

PREPARATION

❑ Supplies vary with project.

PROCEDURE

Bread is a food common to all cultures around the world, symbolizing our common need for sustenance and life. This makes bread a good image to build upon during any church season. The Christian connotation of Jesus as the Bread of Life is easy to see. In addition, during the season of Christmas, the connection can be made to Bethlehem, a word that means "House of Bread." Develop activities using bread as the central focus to nurture the family of faith — at home, at church, or in the community.

- Hold a Christmas bread sale with breads baked by members of the congregation. Use the proceeds to support a hunger project.
- Choose a simple recipe such as pita bread. Make the bread together and then share it during communion.
- Dramatize Bible stories related to bread. Options are the feeding of the 5,000 (Mark 6:30-44); manna in the wilderness (Exodus 16); the widow of Zarephath (1 Kings 17:7-15); and the parable of the leaven (Matthew 13:33).
- Create a church cookbook of bread recipes and share the finished product with each family in the congregation.
- Research traditional Christmas breads from around the world and hold an ethnic celebration to taste the different varieties.
- Encourage treasure hunts through bakeries or church bazaars to collect samples of ethnic breads.
- Hold a potluck featuring foods based on bread: pizza, bowl-shaped bread for soup or salads, tacos, tortillas, cheese breads, sweet breads, and sandwiches.

- Celebrate during a week with breads from all seven continents:
    Sunday: Make corn meal bread or muffins to remember the early staple of North American Native People.
    Monday: Try tortillas and eat a meal like many shared by South Americans each day.
    Tuesday: Buy dark rye or pumpernickel bread like that enjoyed by those of European heritage.
    Wednesday: Purchase or prepare rice cakes and remember the type of grain most common to Asian peoples.
    Thursday: Make chapatis, a common African bread, and use it as spoons for soup or stew.
    Friday: Choose your favorite type of wheat bread (whole, sprouted, cracked, stone-ground, or other) and make some picnic sandwiches like those "down under" in Australia would enjoy in this their summer season.
    Saturday: Create or buy some marbled bread to remind us of the cooperative efforts of those working on scientific experiments in Antarctica, where all food must be imported.
- Bake bread as gifts rather than purchase other expensive trinkets. Add a favorite bread recipe, make a stenciled bread liner, weave a simple basket, or include homemade preserves to complete the gift.
- Eat more simple meals with bread as the staple, and give money saved as a Christmas offering.
- Create bread dough ornaments in shapes to use as tree and home decorations, or to give as gifts.
- Bake a fancy Christmas bread or coffee cake and take it to someone who is housing lots of holiday company.
- Use the "Recipe for the Bread of Life" to include with gifts of home baked bread, or as food for thought in newsletters or bulletins. (Reprinted material must include the following acknowledgment: "Recipe for the Bread of Life," by Anna L. Liechty in Ideas A-Z: Christmas.)

Recipe for the Bread of Life

Begin with three level cups of whole grain truth, stone ground on the tablets of the law.

Sift with wisdom and common sense.

For leavening, add a measure of faith.

Stir in the oil of gladness and sweeten with the love of God, but add the salt from a few tears as well.

Knead and pound the dough with questioning and education until all ingredients are well blended and a consistent texture is achieved.

Place the dough in a warm fellowship of believers to let it rise.

After rising is complete, punch down with adversity and shape the dough into a loaf. It will rise again.

Bake, then, in the fiery furnace of life until golden. When done, break the loaf open and serve generously to others.

Source: The Life of Christ

E: ENVIRONMENT

PURPOSE

To use displays to highlight the message of the Christmas season.

PREPARATION

❑ Supplies vary with project.

PROCEDURE

Highlight the message of the Christmas season with displays in worship spaces, fellowship areas, corridors, entryways, or out-of-doors. Whatever the purpose for the display — to educate, to announce, to celebrate, to honor, to highlight, or to decorate — observe basic rules. Keep exhibits simple and heed fundamental principles of design: consider contrast in color, texture, size and shape. Captions should be brief and easy to read. Studies have shown that displays lose effectiveness after more than five viewings. Enlist the help of church members who are willing to use their time and talent to organize and design special displays.

Following are some hints for varying and simplifying exhibits.

BULLETIN BOARDS

- Cover background with paper tablecloth or fabric appropriate for the season.
- Purchase pre-cut alphabets, stencils or pin-back letters for captions.
- Generate ideas for bulletin boards by looking at bulletin covers, greeting cards, and illustrations in periodicals or curricula.
- Rotate responsibility for bulletin board arrangements. Schedule different classes or groups to sign up for one month.

DISPLAY CASES

- Follow the bulletin board hints.

- Exhibit three-dimensional or fragile items inside a glass enclosure.
- Gather borrowed materials such as antiques, hobbies or other collections related to a religious or seasonal theme. Be sure the case has a lock.
- Create a large diorama to fill the entire space.

SHELVES OR TABLETOPS

- Assemble a collection of items pertaining to a special speaker or event, such as a mission project.
- Arrange objects at different levels. Drape appropriate fabric over blocks or boxes of assorted heights.
- Print captions on "tents" or cards fastened to easels. Use displays to promote a theme or to decorate banquet tables.

CARTONS

- Use large cartons for tabletop displays. Follow tabletop hints.
- Attach announcements or lettering to a tall box for a "kiosk."
- Place an open box on its side to create shadowbox displays.
- Construct carton stair steps or pyramids for an unusual display base.

PIANO

- Anchor heavy fabric or posterboard to the back of an upright piano to create a display background.
- Drape fabric from the top of the piano, across the keys, then over the bench to form a multi-level display area on the front side.

DOORS AND DOORWAYS

- Decorate doors for the current season or exhibit informational materials on door panels or windows.
- Coordinate colors and designs on all of the doors in a corridor to create a unified look.
- Place a small sign on or near each door to identify activities that take place inside the room.
- Fit a tension rod in an open doorway to hang an appropriate banner.

MOBILES, WINDSOCKS AND MORE

- Construct hanging mobiles to include important information or decorative sections.
- Fashion theme-related windsocks to announce upcoming events. Hang them in an entryway or in the church yard.
- String garlands of seasonal materials, time lines or words for decoration or information. Hang computer-generated banners.

PROJECTORS

- Project theme-related transparencies — drawings or announcements — on a blank wall or a screen using an overhead projector.
- Assemble a slide collection and place it in an area for a "do-it-yourself" slide show.

PEOPLE

- Recruit volunteers to wear sandwich boards to advertise events, especially if display space is limited.
- Plan for interactive bulletin boards or displays, allowing individuals to add something to the composition.
- Feature "stars," "Person of the week" or special members from the church family.

WINDOWS AND WINDOWSILLS

- Paint murals or signs on large windows to be viewed from the inside or the outside.
- Create displays in windows with colorful transparent materials such as cellophane or acetate gel sheets.
- Make mini-displays on windowsills or ledges.
- Use window shades for pull-down display space.

F: FIGURES

PURPOSE

To create creche figures from a variety of techniques.

PREPARATION

❏ Supplies vary with project.

PROCEDURE

Nativity sets may range from costly collections to cardboard creations. Yet, regardless of their value in money or memories, or their craft or construction technique, they are all used to tell the story of the events of the birth of the Babe of Bethlehem. Try some of these suggestions for using a creche.

CRECHE CHARACTERS

Purchase or make a Creche Collection to use to prepare for Christmas. Choose one with many figures in the set. Twenty-five suggestions for characters include:

Mary, Joseph, Baby Jesus, Elizabeth, Zechariah, John the Baptist, Gabriel, Caesar, Quirinius, Innkeeper, Shepherds (3), Angels (3), Wise Men (3), Herod, Chief Priest, Scribes (2), Anna, Simeon, Animals.

Set up the stable on the first day of Advent. Add a figure to the scene each day until Christmas. Some of the characters should be set around the scene rather than in the stable. Place the infant in the manger on Christmas Eve or Christmas Day. The three Wise Men should be added on January 6, Epiphany.

CRECHE COLLECTIONS

During the Christmas season, discover the variety of Nativity Sets available and the many materials from which they are made. Look for

Creche Collections representing these methods or materials: Ceramic, Felt, Stained glass, Corn husk, Nails, Blown glass, Cut outs, Crochet, Candles, Sew and stuff, Needlepoint, Wood, Stencil, Stickees, Corrugated cardboard, Clothespins, Decorated toys, Hummel, Ornaments, Cardboard tubes, Stickers, Puppets, Cookies, Clay, Bread dough.

CRECHE CONSTRUCTION

BREAD DOUGH

MATERIALS

- Shoe box
- White bread
- Glue, white
- Cold cream
- Paint, tempera or acrylic
- Brushes
- Mixing bowls or containers
- Water

METHOD

Directions are provided for making creche figures from a bread dough technique. Each batch of bread dough will make about seven three-inch figures.

Remove the crusts from 24 slices of bread. Crumble the bread into a bowl. Add 12 ounces of white glue. Before blending the bread and the glue, the person doing the mixing should rub his or her hands with cold cream. Combine the ingredients and knead the mixture until it's no longer sticky. Divide the dough into two equal balls. One ball, which will remain uncolored, will be used to form the basic creche figures. Color will be added to the second ball and be used for details on the people and animals. Sub-divide the second ball into small pieces. One lump will be needed for each color required. Knead a dab of a different color of paint into each of the small balls.

Form the basic figures — people and animals — for the scene from the uncolored dough.

In another container, mix water and white glue in equal parts. Brush this mixture onto one of the creche figures. Add details such as hair, eyes, clothing, belt and flowers to the figure by making rolls, coils and tiny balls

with the colored dough. Press the features onto the figure and brush the entire finished character with the white glue mixture. Allow the piece to dry. Continue this process until the desired number of people and animals are constructed.

Paint the inside and outside of the shoe box with tempera paint and decorate it to resemble the town of Bethlehem. Use colored dough in the process. Glue the pieces to the box with white glue. Set or glue the figures into the box.

CLAY

MATERIALS

- Clay
- Newspaper
- Wax Paper
- Water
- Paper towels
- Plastic drop cloths
- Tempera paint, optional
- Shellac, optional
- Brushes, optional
- Evergreen branches
- Moss

METHOD

Decide which figures will be made. Take a small amount of clay and form it into the shape of a ball. Work with the clay to sense how it feels and responds. Mold the clay into the desired shapes. Push and pull the clay into figures two to three inches high. Roll clay into a coil to use as arms and add them to the body by using a small amount of water, like glue. Make hair, facial features and decorations with clay, too. Allow the clay to harden. The hardened figures may be painted in bright colors and designs and covered with shellac.

Create a Nativity scene with the newly made figures. Spread evergreen branches and mosses on a table and place the characters in it.

CLOTHES PINS

MATERIALS

- Wooden clothes pins with rounded tops
- Pipe cleaners
- Fabric scraps
- Yarn
- Scissors
- Markers
- Shoe box
- Construction paper
- Straw or sand

METHOD

Create a creche to use throughout the Christmas season by constructing figures from wooden clothes pins. For each figure, draw a face on the head or rounded top of the clothespin. Twist a pipe cleaner around the neck to form arms. Cut a two inch by six inch rectangle of fabric. Fold it in half and cut a small slit in the center. Slide the head through the opening. Arrange the material over the arms. Secure it in place by tying a piece of yarn around the middle. Hair may be formed from yarn and glued to the top of the clothespin. A small piece of cloth may be draped over the top of the head and tied in place with yarn. Construct a variety of characters including Mary, Joseph, Jesus, Shepherds and angels.

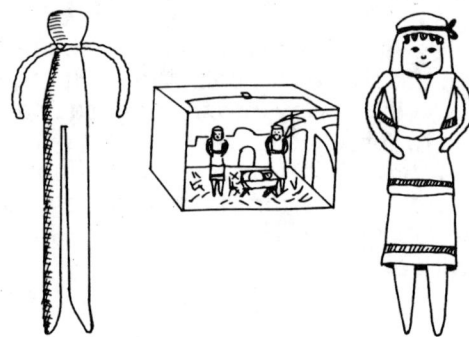

Form the stable by covering the shoe box with construction paper. Set it on its side and sprinkle the bottom with straw or sand. Place all of the characters in and around it.

COOKIE DOUGH

MATERIALS

- 1/3 cup shortening
- 1/3 cup sugar
- 1 egg
- 2/3 cup honey
- 1 teaspoon lemon flavoring
- 2 3/4 cups flour

- ☐ 1 teaspoon baking soda
- ☐ 1 teaspoon salt
- ☐ Cookie cutters
- ☐ Mixing and baking utensils and equipment
- ☐ Frosting
- ☐ Decorations
- ☐ Ribbon

METHOD

Create a cookie dough creche, hang the pieces as ornaments on a tree, and share the results with family and friends during and after the holiday season.

Mix shortening, sugar, egg, honey and flavoring thoroughly. Stir together flour, baking soda, salt and blend into the shortening mixture. Chill dough. Heat oven to 375 degrees. Roll dough out 1/4 inch thick. Cut into desired shapes. Use cookie cutters to make the shapes, or find pictures of the characters in used Sunday School material, coloring books or flannel graph sets, and make patterns from them. Poke a hole into the top of each cookie so ribbon may be strung through it later. Place cookies one-inch apart on a lightly greased baking sheet. Bake eight to ten minutes. When cool, ice and decorate as desired. Thread a piece of ribbon through the hole in the top of each cookie and use it to hang as an ornament on the tree.

For molasses cookies, use brown sugar in place of granulated sugar, molasses for honey, and two teaspoons cinnamon and one teaspoon ginger for lemon flavoring.

PIPE CLEANERS

MATERIALS

- ☐ Construction paper scraps
- ☐ Fabric scraps
- ☐ Pipe cleaners or chenille wires
- ☐ Cardboard pieces
- ☐ Crayons, markers or paints
- ☐ Brushes
- ☐ Scissors
- ☐ Glue
- ☐ Tape
- ☐ Table

METHOD

Construct and display items representing the Christmas story and present them in a table top model in the home or church. Form the figures of people and animals by bending and shaping the pipe cleaners. Add fabric and construction paper scraps to the chenille wire to make faces and clothing. Create animals using the same procedure.

In keeping with the customs of many cultures, include people from all walks of life in the creche. Remember that the Christ Child welcomes everyone. Depict people from different countries in the scene too.

Place the characters on the top of a table. Decide on the type of scene that will surround the figures and create it from materials with interesting textures and shapes. Add trees, hills, water, buildings and anything else that would enhance the model.

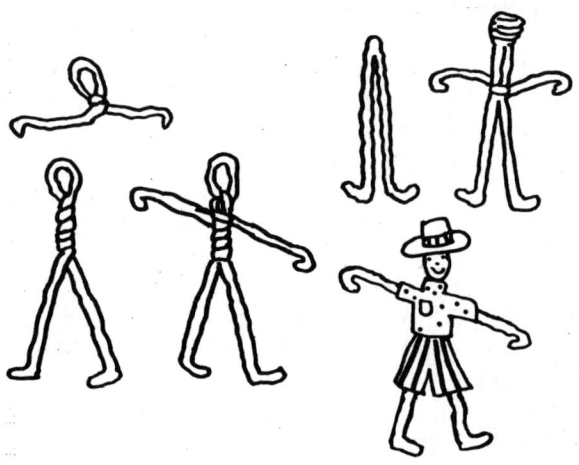

G: GREENS

PURPOSE

To offer ideas for "Hanging of the Greens."

PREPARATION

❑ Supplies vary with project.

PROCEDURE

"Hanging of the Greens" dates back to pagan times when holly, ivy, and other greenery were used to decorate for winter festivals. Many varieties of evergreens are found throughout the world; because evergreens flourish year-round and holly bears fruit in the winter, these plants have become symbols of eternal life. Many of the ancient legends became intertwined with Christian symbolism. Some of the characteristics attributed to the greens include cedar, tree of royalty — used for purification; pine, fir, yew and cypress — denote living forever; mistletoe — identifies with healing properties and sign of peace; holly leaves and berries — symbolize Jesus' crown of thorns and droplets of blood; and ivy — represents love, growth and endurance. The wreath, a circle of greens, signifies the eternal kingdom of Jesus, the Christ.

The traditional time for "hanging of the greens" is the first Sunday of Advent. In preparation for the coming of Christ, it is fitting to have garlands, boughs, trees, and wreaths to remind us of God's gift of eternal life. Plan a special worship service or other activity to beautify the church. Ideas include:

- Design a Sunday morning worship service around symbols for Advent, including information about evergreens. Bless the greens, decorate the sanctuary as part of the worship service, light the Advent wreath and choose appropriate Scripture and hymns.
- Hold a special worship service to feature the physical preparation as well as the spiritual preparation for the season. The service

should take place on the Saturday before Advent begins or on the first Sunday of Advent, in the afternoon or evening.

- Organize an intergenerational event to decorate the entire building. Designate areas to be decorated by different classes or groups. Rotate assignments each year. End with a combined worship service.
- Plan an Advent workshop to fashion garlands, wreaths, and a variety of ornaments to use in decorating the church halls, classrooms and sanctuary. For an attractive display, follow a theme or coordinate colors and materials.
- Expand the workshop to include the making of an Advent wreath to be used at home. Provide devotional materials to use with the wreath. Make wreaths and worship booklets to share with shut-ins.
- Arrange for a special program to coincide with the "hanging of the greens," such as a concert, drama, puppet show or other family entertainment. Consider refreshments or a light meal as part of the celebration and invite all ages to participate.

Whether the "hanging of the greens" is an informal event or a sacred service, all of the symbolism and beauty of the evergreens help us to prepare for the Christmas season.

H: HYMN STORY

PURPOSE

To use the hymn, "Prepare The Way Of The Lord," and a cylinder stamp teaching tool to emphasize the message of Christmas.

PREPARATION

- ❑ Music for "Prepare The Way Of The Lord", Taize
- ❑ Liquid tempera paint or finger paint
- ❑ Shallow pans
- ❑ Cylinders such as rolling pins, juice cans, pop cans, spools, cardboard tubes
- ❑ Yarn
- ❑ String
- ❑ Glue
- ❑ Scissors
- ❑ Posterboard, sponge, self-adhesive in-soles
- ❑ Construction paper
- ❑ Paper towels
- ❑ Newspaper

PROCEDURE

"Prepare the Way Of The Lord," a hymn by Jacques Berthier and the community of Taize, France is based on Scripture passages from the Old and New Testaments: Isaiah 40:3, Isaiah 52:10, and Matthew 3:3. The song emphasizes the theme that the repetition of the message of Christmas creates a common language of praise among God's people. Create a cylinder stamp teaching tool, use the dialogue provided, and share this important point.

INSTRUCTIONS FOR CREATING THE CYLINDER STAMP

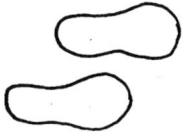 

Printing a design is a fun way to create an illustration of feet to use as the teaching tool for the song "Prepare The Way Of The Lord." A simple way to make the "prints" is to form designs on cylinders and roll them across paper.

Select a cylinder to use for the project. Cut foot "prints" from posterboard, sponge, or adhesive backed in-soles and attach them to the cylinder. The stamps may also be created by gluing yarn or string to the base to form the footprint shapes.

Pour each color of paint into a shallow container. Select a piece of paper for the project and fold it in half to form a card. Roll the tube in the paint. Roll the cylinder across the paper. This may be done several times to create a repeated pattern. Allow the paint to dry.

SUGGESTIONS FOR DIALOGUE AND DISCUSSION

[Let the participants see or create the footprint pattern.] Isn't it amazing that we can create all these footprints from just the few on this roller! Once we create the pattern, it isn't difficult at all to make as many footprints as we'd like. Here I have used the footprint stamp to make the border of a Christmas card. [Hold up sample card.] Do footprints seem a strange shape to use on a Christmas card? [Discuss what is more usual — bells, stars, trees.] Well, these footprints can help us understand the special message of the Christmas song we sing called "Prepare the Way of the Lord."

The words are taken from the Bible, from the prophecy of Isaiah. The song itself was written not too long ago by Jacques Berthier and a group of Christians in France called the Taize Community. Christians from all over the world travel to France to visit the community and join in their simple ways of worship and prayer. These footsteps can remind us first of the many people who find their way to the Taize Community.

One of the ways the community worships is by repeating words from Scripture in simple songs. The repetition of sacred phrases, like the repetition of the stamp, creates a pattern of praise that connects the worshipers. Isaiah's words in this song remind us to "prepare the way of the Lord" so that "all people will see the salvation of our God." These words were also repeated by John the Baptist before Jesus began His ministry.

We can get ready for Christmas if we "prepare the way of the Lord" by worshiping and focusing our thoughts on the importance of Jesus' birth. And when we prepare ourselves for a meaningful Christmas, we become better messengers to others so that they hear the Good News of Christ's love. Now that's a message worth repeating!

I: INTERGENERATIONAL

PURPOSE

To use "Christmas Around The World" as the theme of an all-church event.

PREPARATION

❑ Supplies vary with project.

PROCEDURE

"Joy To The World! The Lord is come!" The words of this familiar carol proclaim that Christmas is a worldwide celebration. Christians on all continents commemorate the birth of the Savior in countless ways: picnics on sunny beaches in Australia; presents surrounding decorated trees in Germany; printed postcards exchanged in Japan; posada processions through villages of Mexico; pageants that portray the nativity in Nigeria; plates filled with delicacies from smorgasbord tables in Sweden.

Celebrate Christmas with an event to help the entire Sunday School — and even the entire congregation — explore and experience some of the ways in which Christ's birth is commemorated around the world. Use this unique design — Gather! Explore! Celebrate! Share! — during one or more church school sessions, as a special children's or intergenerational program, or as an exciting educational event during Christmas break.

GATHER!

Gather the participants in the sanctuary for music and an explanation of the program. Sing carols with international origins, such as: "From Heaven Above To Earth I Come" (Germany), "Infant Holy, Infant Lowly" (Poland); "Joyful Christmas Day Is Here" (Japan); "O Holy Night" (France), "The First Noel" (England), and "Silent Night" (Austria). Besides congregational singing, music may be presented by choirs, soloists, small groups, and instrumentalists.

EXPLORE!

Continue the event in a large room, such as a social hall, or in individual classrooms, where a variety of "Christmas Around The World" learning activities have been prepared in advance. Displays related to international customs may also be exhibited.

AUSTRALIA — STORY

ACTIVITY

Flannel graph Figures

MATERIALS

- Felt
- Flannel background
- Glue
- Markers
- <u>The Nativity</u> (Vivas, Julie, Illustrator. San Diego: Harcourt Brace Jovanovich, 1986.)
- Paper
- Pellon interfacing
- Pencils
- Sandpaper
- Scissors
- Bible story books

METHOD

Australian illustrator Julie Vivas captures the spirit of the Christmas story in a lovely picture book, <u>The Nativity</u>. The text uses excerpts from the Bible and the pictures illustrate the events that took place when the Savior was born. Read the book or look at the pictures. Make flannel graph pieces of some of the characters and use them to tell the story. Prepare patterns for the main characters of the book by drawing them freehand, or tracing the illustrations. Copy the figures onto the interfacing material. Color and highlight the pieces and cut them out. Back the shapes with small pieces of sandpaper or felt so they will adhere to the background material. Place the figures on the background at the appropriate times in the story.

BRAZIL — CRAFTS

ACTIVITY

Tissue Paper Flowers

MATERIALS

- Floral Tape, green
- Florist wire
- Pencils

- ❏ Paper
- ❏ Petal Patterns
- ❏ Scissors
- ❏ Tissue Paper, various colors

METHOD

Crafts from Brazil reflect the influence of the country's Native, European and African inhabitants. Bold sculpture, beautiful carvings, and brilliant paintings are found both indoors and outside. Directions are provided for a craft project, tissue paper flowers, that will serve as a reminder of the culture and customs of Brazil. The flowers suggest the bright blossoms that bloom during the Christmas season. Make one or more flowers in different colors and sizes. Use them as table or tree decorations.

Trace the petal patterns and enlarge or reduce them to the desired size. Cut the petals from various colors of tissue paper. For a fuller flower, cut two or three of each petal. Put the decorations together in order, with number one as the base of the flower. Cut a piece of florist's wire 12" long. Beginning underneath the base of the flower, run the wire up through the center of all the petals, then back down in the center to form a small loop. Twist the two pieces of wire together and cover the stem with green floral tape.

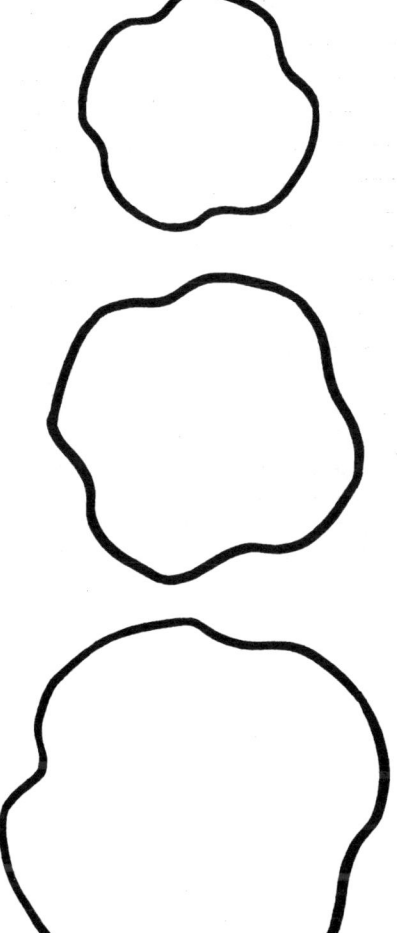
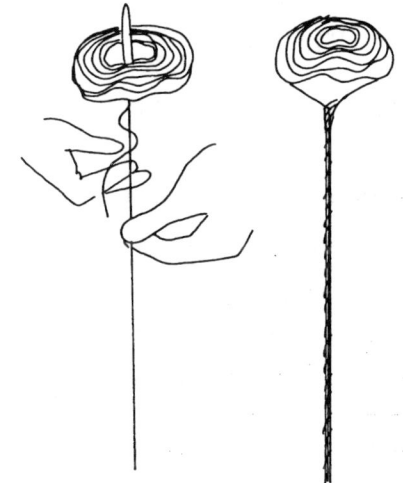

CANADA (FRENCH) - CARD

ACTIVITY

Stained Glass Window Design

MATERIALS

- ❏ Construction paper, black and various colors;

- ❑ Glue or glue sticks;
- ❑ Markers;
- ❑ Scissors;
- ❑ Tape;
- ❑ Tissue paper.

METHOD

Stained glass is an art form in which pieces of tinted glass are assembled in a lead frame to form a picture or design. Daylight or artificial light that passes through the glass is transformed into an array of color. Stained glass windows, found in the great cathedrals of the world, often depict scenes from Bible stories. Topics related to the Christmas story include Madonna and Child, Holy Family, Adoration of the Shepherds, and the Visit of the Magi. Follow the directions and make a Christmas card that resembles a stained glass window.

Begin with a square of black construction paper. Fold it corner to corner to form a triangle. Cut a circle out of the paper. With the black paper still folded into the triangle shape, or smaller, cut a design such as a star or a snowflake. Remember to cut on the folds as well as on the edge of the black paper. Unfold the paper. Glue or tape colored tissue paper pieces behind each opening of the design. Fold a piece of construction paper in half and glue the stained glass piece to the front of it. Write a message on the inside of the card before it is delivered or mailed.

ECUADOR — GREETINGS

ACTIVITY

Ribbon Banner

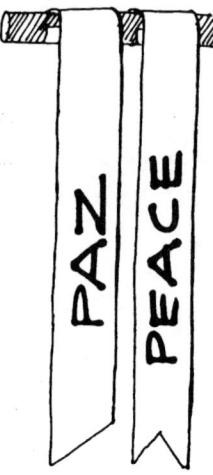

MATERIALS

- ❑ Permanent markers
- ❑ Ribbon
- ❑ Rods or straws
- ❑ Scissors
- ❑ Tape
- ❑ String or yarn

METHOD

Since Spanish is the official language of Ecuador the greeting of the season is *Feliz Navidad*. The greeting of peace is *paz*. Create a ribbon banner as a way to remember the greetings and the people of Ecuador.

Choose ribbon to use for the activity. Cut three pieces of ribbon six inches long. With permanent marker, write the word "ECUADOR" on one ribbon, the Spanish greeting of the season "FELIZ NAVIDAD" on the second, and the word peace "PAZ" on the third. Tape or glue the tops of each ribbon to one rod. Form a hanger for the ribbon banner by attaching a length of yarn or string to each side of the rod.

INDIA — GAME

ACTIVITY

Matching Game

MATERIALS

- ❑ Games
- ❑ Pencils

METHOD

Play a matching game featuring some of the Christmas customs and traditions of India. Draw a line from the statement with a number to the word below with a letter that best answers or describes each phrase.

GAME

1. One of the many religions found in India.
2. Method used to present the Gospel story on Christmas Eve.
3. Brightly colored plant used as a holiday decoration.
4. White banner with a red cross in the center.
5. Lines the roofs of Christian homes on Christmas Eve.
6. Opportunity to invite non-Christian friends and family to church.
7. Follows the Christmas Eve worship service.
8. Traditional gift at Christmas.
9. Method of applying wax and dyes to create works of art.
10. Spice used in many Indian foods.

A. Poinsettia
B. Candles
C. Clothing
D. Curry
E. Worship Service
F. Hindu
G. Party
H. Christmas flag
I. Batik
J. Drama

ANSWERS

1. F   2. J   3. A   4. H   5. B   6. E   7. G   8. C   9. I   10. D

MEXICO - GIFT GIVER

ACTIVITY

Tube Puppet

MATERIALS

- Paper tubes
- Felt
- Yarn or fake fur
- Fabric scraps
- Scissors
- Glue
- Craft sticks or dowel rods

METHOD

In Mexico small gifts for children are left at the manger scene on Christmas morning. The real gifts are given by the Three Kings on Epiphany, January 6. On the night of January 5, children fill their shoes with straw from the manger and leave it as an offering for the camels. In the morning, the straw is gone and the shoes are buried in mounds of gifts. Make a Wise Man puppet and tell the story of the Gift Giver of Mexico.

Select a paper tube, which can be any size. Form the puppet face by cutting a piece of felt and gluing it to the top one-third of the tube. Make facial features from felt scraps and glue them in place. Yarn or fake fur becomes hair and should be attached to the top of the tube.

Glue a piece of felt around the remainder of the tube to serve as the undergarment. Layers of fabric in contrasting or complementary colors can be added as over-garments.

Make arms from strips of cloth or felt and glue them to the sides of the tube.

Apply a craft stick to the inside back of the tube to serve as the rod by which the puppet is operated.

If felt is not available, use construction paper instead. The facial features may be drawn on with marker. Substitute tissue paper for fabric to form the outer garments.

NIGERIA — CUSTOMS

ACTIVITY

Video box mural

MATERIALS

- Cardboard carton
- Knife
- Dowel rods
- Paper
- Markers
- Tape

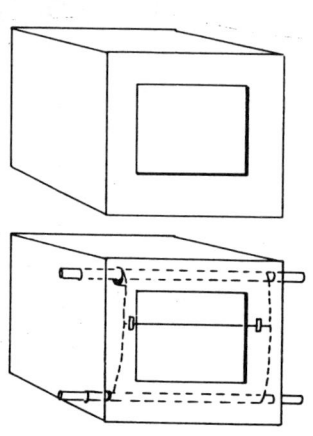

42

❑ Cardboard or wood scraps

METHOD

Approximately forty percent of the one hundred fifteen million inhabitants of Nigeria are Christians. The birthday of the Savior is an occasion for great joy and celebration. It is customary for Nigerians to wear new clothes on Christmas. For men and boys it could be shirts and trousers, or robes and hats, while women generally wear a blouse and body wrap of colorful fabric and a brightly patterned head tie. Church services on Christmas involve large pageants with many scenes. Worship services and programs provide wonderful ways to celebrate the gospel story and to share the good news with non-Christian relatives and friends, many of whom practice Islam or tribal religions. Although giving gifts is not as popular in Nigeria as it is in the United States, people tend to go from house to house, similar to trick or treating, in the hopes of getting candy or coins. Singing and dancing are part of all festive occasions in Africa, and Christmas is no exception.

Use a video box to share some of the Christmas customs of Nigeria. A video box combines a series of drawings that tell a story with a method for showing them that is similar to a television screen. The box may range in size from a tiny matchbox to a huge cardboard carton. The instructions below are for a large box that can display many drawings. Begin by tucking in or cutting off the flaps of the carton. Use a mat knife to cut a large square out of the center of the bottom of the box. Leave a 2" or 3" border around the entire area. Turn the box on its side, so that the bottom now becomes the front, or viewing area.

Make a set of parallel holes in the top and bottom of the box on both sides of the window. Place a dowel rod through each set of holes. Secure them in place with tape or a cardboard or wooden stop. Use markers to illustrate each custom on individual sheets of paper. When the drawings are completed, tape them together to form a long roll. Attach the beginning of the mural to one dowel rod and the end to the other. Wind the mural through the box to tell the story.

POLAND - CAROLS

ACTIVITY

Look at and listen to music

MATERIALS

❑ Earphones
❑ Record jackets
❑ Book and tape of Polish Christmas carols
❑ Tape player

METHOD

Over fifty Polish carols complete with accompaniment, traditional tunes and new arrangements, are included in the book <u>Treasured Polish</u>

Christmas Customs And Traditions (Minneapolis: Polanie Publishing Company, 1971. Order from the Polish Museum Gift Shop, 984 N. Milwaukee Ave., Chicago, IL 60622 or call 800-772-8632. $16.95 plus $2.00 shipping). Most of the songs are printed with English and Polish words. Read and review the Polish Christmas carols contained in the book. Look at the record jackets and tape cases to discover more about Polish carols. Listen to the tape of Polish Christmas music.

SWEDEN — CRECHE

ACTIVITY

Acorn and Pinecone creche figures

MATERIALS

- ❏ Acorns
- ❏ Pine cones
- ❏ Knife
- ❏ Glue
- ❏ Scissors
- ❏ Construction paper
- ❏ Fabric scraps
- ❏ Yarn
- ❏ Permanent markers
- ❏ Straw

METHOD

In keeping with the Swedish people's use of natural materials, construct a Nativity set out of acorns and pine cones. If the pine cones are large, cut them in half. For each creche figure, glue an acorn on top of a pinecone half. Allow the pieces to dry thoroughly.

Decorate the figures with cloth, construction paper and yarn. Cut a circular strip of fabric for each costume. Wrap a piece of material around each pinecone and glue it in place. Small pieces of yarn may be glued to the tops of the acorns to form hair. Triangles can be cut and glued to the hair to make headpieces. Cut arms from construction paper and glue them to the top portion of the costumes. Eyes or other facial features may be drawn on the acorns with permanent marker.

Make the baby Jesus by wrapping a small piece of cloth or paper around an acorn. Glue it in place.

At a later time create a Nativity scene on a table or in a box. Spread out the straw and set the figures on it.

CELEBRATE!

At the conclusion of the activity time, form a procession, and journey from the social hall to the sanctuary for a time of worship including carols, Scripture, prayer and a brief devotion.

SHARE!

Following worship, invite the participants to the social hall to share refreshments or a meal. Feature desserts and dishes from around the world.

J: JESSE TREE

PURPOSE

To trace the roots of personal faith in Jesus.

PREPARATION

- ❑ Pencils or pens
- ❑ Scissors
- ❑ Tree branches
- ❑ Coffee cans
- ❑ Ribbon, string or yarn
- ❑ Stones
- ❑ Fabric or foil
- ❑ Construction paper or felt
- ❑ Glue
- ❑ Paper clips
- ❑ Punch

PROCEDURE

Frequently used during the season of Advent, the four-week period preceding Christmas, the "Jesse Tree" incorporates symbols that recall important people and events which are a significant part of Jesus' ancestry. A "Jesse Tree" is much like a family tree, and is named for the Father of David, who lived about one thousand years before Jesus. The prophecy predicting the coming of the "Branch of Jesse" is found in Isaiah 11.

Traditionally, symbols on a "Jesse Tree" correspond to stories recorded in Old and New Testament Scripture passages. Each event or person prepared the world for Jesus in a unique way. As an Advent devotional guide, use the "Jesse Tree" format from December 1 through December 24 to trace the roots of your belief in Jesus. Add the names of twenty-four people who have shaped your faith and use this personal approach to prepare anew for Christ's coming on Christmas day, December 25.

Prepare a base for the "Faith Tree". Cover a large coffee can with a piece of fabric or foil. Tie ribbon around the top of the material to hold it in place. Set the tree branch in the center of the can and fill the container with stones to anchor the limb. This will serve as the base which will hold the symbols that trace the roots of your faith in Jesus.

Cut shapes out of felt or construction paper. Add the name of a significant person on your faith journey every day for twenty-four days. Include people such as: mother, father, grandmother, grandfather, sister, brother, husband, wife, son, daughter, pastor, elementary school teacher, high school teacher, college instructor, Sunday School teacher, youth group leader, neighbor, co-worker, camp counselor, choir director, Christian Educator director, mid-week program coordinator, friend, catechism teacher, and even stranger. Add details with marker drawings, photos and illustrations, or decorative trims.

Poke a hole at the top of each symbol and attach an opened paper clip to serve as an ornament hanger. Choose a different symbol each day — in chronological order — and connect it to the branch. Complete the activity by looking up Bible passages on faith.

Display the unique "tree" as a reminder of your personal connection to Jesus.

K: KIDS

PURPOSE

To share a story of the Good News of God's love.

PREPARATION

- ❑ Book of legends
- ❑ Donkey (ceramic or plastic figure, stuffed animal, or wood cut-out)

PROCEDURE

Kids, of all ages, love stories! Share the Christmas legend of "The Little Grey Donkey" as the Children's Message in a worship service or program or as a teaching tale in a classroom or family night setting.

"The Little Grey Donkey"

[Hold up a book of Christmas legends.] This is a book of Christmas legends. Do you know what a legend is? *[Wait for possible ideas before explaining.]* A legend is a story that contains some truth, but has some made-up parts, too. This book is full of made-up stories about Christmas. Many of the Christmas legends are about animals, and they make wonderful stories to help us get ready for the birth of Jesus. Part of the challenge of the holidays is to sort out the truth from the pretend. Interestingly enough, legends — stories built on our imaginations — can help us discover what is real and what is important.

One legend of Christmas is about the donkey that carried Mary to Bethlehem when Jesus was born. He was an old, grey, pitiful donkey. His owner didn't want him anymore because the donkey was blind, and not being able to see made him even more stubborn than donkeys usually were. The owner decided to get rid of him.

At this same time, Joseph had to obey an order to return to his family's home town to register for the Roman tax. He needed some way to take

Mary on the long journey because she was expecting a baby, and she couldn't walk all that way. Unfortunately, Joseph didn't have much money to buy a horse or cart. The donkey's owner laughingly offered his old, blind donkey to Joseph, who gladly accepted such a gift. Tenderly, Joseph placed his expectant wife on the little gray donkey's back.

Now, that donkey could have used its big ears to listen to all the scary noises out in the desert. He could have planted his feet and refused to move. In fact, that's what the original owner expected to happen. But instead, Joseph spoke so lovingly, so kindly and reassuringly, that the little donkey stepped out in faith to follow the sound of his new master's voice. He allowed himself to be led all the way to Bethlehem.

Isn't that a wonderful legend? Is that story in the Bible? Well, no. In fact, the Bible doesn't even say that Mary rode on a donkey. Over the years, people have used their imaginations to picture the story of the holy family traveling to Bethlehem. They must have traveled somehow. It isn't unrealistic to imagine that Mary rode on a donkey, is it?

Although the legend of the blind donkey is based largely on imagination, the story is built on important truth. God is our loving leader. We can trust God even when we can't see what lies ahead. Like the little donkey, we must take steps of faith to follow God's voice as we find our way to the manger of Bethlehem. There we will find not a legend, but the reality of Jesus, our Savior.

Let's ask God to help us be good listeners so we can hear the Good News of God's message of love.

PRAYER

[Invite the children to repeat each phrase of the prayer.]
Good morning, God. Help us to listen and follow in faith as You lead us to Christmas. Amen.

L: LIGHT

PURPOSE

To use learning activities related to light to illustrate the theme of Christmas.

PREPARATION

❑ Supplies vary with project.

PROCEDURE

Light plays a significant part in the Christmas season. In the following activities, participants will create candles, fashion candle holders, or design items which let in light. Use lighted candles with adult supervision.

BEESWAX CANDLE

Check craft or hobby stores for sheets of beeswax and wicking. Place one piece of the honeycomb on the work surface and lay a strip of wick along the edge of the sheet. Cut the wick long enough to extend beyond the side you wish to roll up. Fold the wax over the wick and press it down to hold the wick in place. Roll up the candle. Cut out symbols or shapes from contrasting colors of beeswax and press gently onto the candle to decorate. Larger pillars can be formed by rolling more than one sheet around the wick.

DECORATED CANDLE

Choose a white or ivory pillar candle. Cut pictures or symbols from paper napkins or gift wrap with an appropriate seasonal motif. Brush white craft glue onto the side of the candle and carefully apply the napkin design or illustration. Smooth out paper with fingers or brush a small amount of thinned glue over the surface. For a quick and easy method, use stickers to decorate the candles.

SAND CANDLE

Fill a large bowl or box with sand. Dampen the sand in the center so that the hole you dig holds its shape. Scoop out sand in a free form or in a star pattern. To fill a 4" by 4" depression, you will need 1/2 pound of melted paraffin or old candles. For the wick, anchor a candle stub in the center of the hole. Trim the stub so it is level with the top of the hole, allowing the wick to extend above the sand. Melt the candle pieces or paraffin chunks in the top of a double boiler. It will take 10 to 15 minutes for 1/2 pound of wax to melt. Have adult supervision at all times for this project, as wax burns easily! To add color, stir in one or two broken crayons. Use extreme caution when pouring the wax into the depression in the sand. Allow the wax to cool and to shrink for about 15 minutes, then add some more hot wax. Let the wax harden for several hours. Dig the candle out of the mold and dust off any loose sand. Cut or scrape the candle so the bottom will be flat.

SHELL LAMP

Form another molded candle by pouring melted wax into a sea shell. In order for the shell to have a level base, glue on a plastic drapery ring or feet made of marbles or beads. Place a tea light candle in a scallop or cockle shell, then fill the hollow with wax.

PIERCED TIN CAN LANTERN

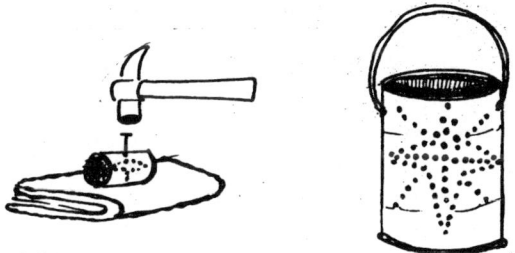

Choose food cans with smooth sides for the best lanterns. Wash can, remove label and dry carefully. File any sharp edges. Draw symbols or designs around the can using a permanent marker to make dotted lines. Fill the can with water and place it in the freezer for 24 hours so it can freeze solid. In order to pierce the design, lay the can on its side on a folded towel. With a hammer and a nail, follow along the dots to form the perforations. Tap just hard enough to pierce the metal. Use nails of different sizes to add variety to the pattern. If ice begins to melt, return the can to the freezer for a few hours. When the design is finished, set the can in the sink or a dishpan to melt the ice. Dry the outside of the can, but allow the jagged inside to air dry. Use tongs to place a votive candle in the bottom of the can. Long matches or a lighted taper will be a safe way to light the lantern. Adult supervision is required.

GLASS AND FOIL LANTERN

Select a small jar with straight sides. Cut a piece of heavy duty foil and a strip of brightly-colored tissue paper long enough to wrap around the jar. Cut the foil so it is about one inch taller than the container; fold under 1/2 inch along the top and bottom edges. Use a blunt pencil to draw simple pictures or symbols across the foil. Follow along the pattern with a hole punch. Wrap the tissue paper around the jar and fasten with a little white glue. Cover the tissue with the punched foil and tape it at the seam to keep it from slipping. Place a votive candle in the bottom of the lantern. The candlelight will shine through the colored tissue.

PERFORATED PAPER DESIGNS

Create luminaries by cutting or punching openings in paper bags. The openwork designs may be repeat patterns or simple shapes. Fold down the top edge of the bag to form a cuff, then pour two or more inches of sand in the bottom of the luminary. Push a candle stub into the sand to hold it firmly in place and be certain each candle is away from the sides of the bag. Use caution when lighting the candles and appoint someone to monitor them during the time they will be burning. An alternative plan would be to use flashlights instead of lighted candles.

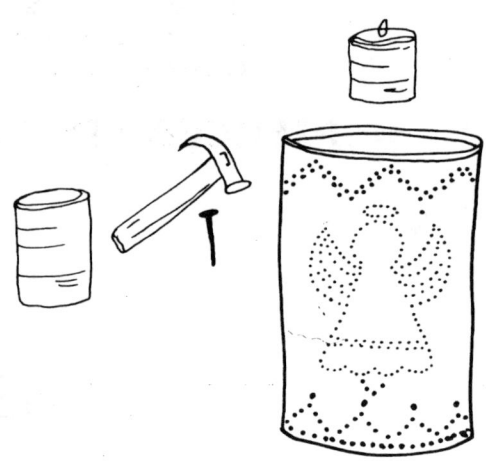

Another project fashioned from perforated paper is a simple lamp shade. Make a pattern by wrapping thin paper around an existing lamp shade. Mark and trim it to fit, then trace the pattern onto vellum or parchment-type paper. Plan a design of symbols or shapes with light pencil lines. Use a craft knife or hole punch to create openings in the paper. Carefully wrap the perforated paper around the shade. Glue the paper in place if the cover will be permanent; pin the paper for a temporary cover. Use care when cutting with a craft knife and when handling lamp shades.

FLASHLIGHT ACTIVITY

Look in resource materials for information about constellations. Mark the formation of a constellation in the center of a circle of black construction paper, then punch out the "stars" with the point of a pencil. Wrap the paper over the end of a flashlight. Hold in place with a rubber band. Turn on the flashlight and shine the constellation on the ceiling of a darkened room. Try different star formations.

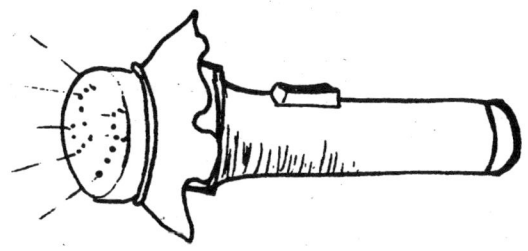

SUN

Purchase packages of light-sensitive photography paper to make sun prints. Kits are available at craft, hobby or photo stores. View rainbows produced by sunlight through a prism.

PROJECTORS

Use an overhead projector to experiment with light shining through transparent materials such as containers of colored water, acetate sheets, or outlines on transparencies. Create shadows or silhouettes with the strong beam from a slide or filmstrip projector.

HOUSEHOLD LIGHTS

List all of the places in the home that have some type of light: lamps, ceiling lights, refrigerator, oven, computer, dryer, alarm clock, and so forth.

M: MUSIC

PURPOSE

To provide an opportunity to experience the Christmas story through music.

PREPARATION

- Music for selected songs
- Accompaniment

PROCEDURE

For many people a highlight of the Christmas season is singing songs associated with the holiday. Use this program design to tell the Christmas story through song and Scripture. As a unique approach, feature people of different ages playing selections on brass, woodwind, string, and percussion instruments. This is a great program for children to prepare for parents or for young people to present to older folks. It also works well as a devotional for a family night activity or a women's, men's or small group meeting. Nurture the family of faith through Christmas music at home, at church, or in the community.

Call To Worship *[Read responsively]*

One: Sing for joy, O heavens, and exult, O earth; break forth, O mountains, into singing! For the Lord has comforted His people, and will have compassion on His suffering ones. (Isaiah 49:15)

All: I will be glad and exult in you; I will sing praise to your name, O Most High. (Psalm 9:2)

One: Sing and rejoice, O daughter of Zion; for lo, I will come and dwell in your midst, says the Lord. (Zechariah 2:10)

All: Glory to God in the highest heaven, and on earth peace among those whom he favors! (Luke 2:14)

Congregational Hymn: "There's A Song In The Air"

Reading: Luke 2:1, 3-5
In those days a decree went out from Emperor Augustus that all the world should be registered. All went to their own towns to be registered. Joseph also went from the town of Nazareth in Galilee to Judea, to the city of David called Bethlehem, because he was descended from the house and family of David. He went to be registered with Mary, to whom he was engaged and who was expecting a child.

Flute Duet: "O Little Town Of Bethlehem"

Reading: Luke 2:6-7
While they were there, the time came for her to deliver her child. And she gave birth to her firstborn son and wrapped him in bands of cloth, and laid him in a manger, because there was no place for them in the inn.

Piano Solos: "Silent Night," "O Holy Night"

Reading: Luke 2:8
And in that region there were shepherds, keeping watch over their flock by night.

Saxophone Solo: "While Shepherds Watched Their Flock By Night"

Reading: Luke 2:9
Then an angel of the Lord stood before them, and the glory of the Lord shone around them, and they were terrified.

Flute Duet:
"It Came Upon The Midnight Clear"

Reading: Luke 2:10-12
But the angel said to them, "Do not be afraid; for see — I am bringing you good news of great joy for all the people: to you is born this day in the city of David a Savior, who is the Messiah, the Lord. This will be a sign for you: you will find a child wrapped in bands of cloth and lying in a manger."

Trumpet Solo: "The First Noel"

Reading: Luke 2:13,14
And suddenly there was with the angel a multitude of the heavenly host, praising God and saying, "Glory to God in the highest heaven, and on earth peace among those whom he favors!"

Congregational Hymn: "Angels, From the Realms of Glory"

Organ Solo: "Angels We Have Heard On High"

Reading: Luke 2:15,16
When the angels had left them and gone into heaven, the shepherds said to one another, "Let us go now to Bethlehem and see this thing that has taken place, which the Lord has made known to us." So they went ... and found Mary and Joseph, and the child lying in the manger.

Piano Solo: "O Come All Ye Faithful"

Reading: Luke 2:17
When they saw this, they made known what had been told them about this child.

Organ Solo: "Ring The Bells"

Reading: Matthew 2:1,2,11
Wise men from the East came to Jerusalem, asking, "Where is the child who has been born king of the Jews? For we observed his star, and have come to pay him homage." On entering the house, they saw the child with Mary his mother; and they knelt down and paid him homage. Then, opening their treasure chests, they offered him gifts of gold, frankincense, and myrrh.

Trumpet Solo: "We Three Kings"

Prayer

Congregational Hymn: "Joy To The World"

Doxology: "While Shepherds Watched Their Flocks" - Verse 6

N: NURTURE

PURPOSE

To offer information for bulletins, take-home letters, and newsletter articles to help "Nurture Faith" during the Christmas season.

PREPARATION

- ❏ "Come To Your Senses" suggestions
- ❏ Duplicating equipment
- ❏ Paper

PROCEDURE

In the church we often emphasize the mission Jesus calls us to saying, "Go into all the world." However, we must remember that Jesus' first word to the disciples was "Come." Nurture is perhaps the first and most important commitment of the church to its flock: shepherding, training, educating — in a word, "discipling." The seasons of Advent, Christmas, and Epiphany — the beginning of the Christian story — are good times to gather in and nurture those in our congregations.

The following suggestions may be used as insert information for bulletins, take-home letters, and newsletters; or the ideas may be further developed into a planned program of nurture during one or all of the seasons. The emphasis is on allowing faith to "Come to Our Senses."

"COME TO YOUR SENSES"

LISTEN

Scripture: Isaiah 55:3a

Advent—Listen for God during Advent by learning a new way to pray. Instead of closing and folding hands in prayer, hold palms up and open during quiet time.

Christmas—Listen for the gift of loving words during the Christmas season. Instead of brushing compliments or praise aside, receive the words with humility as gifts from God.

Epiphany—Listen for new ideas with an open mind. Tune in a Christian radio or television program to hear how God's love is being revealed in the world.

BREATHE

Scripture: Job 33:4

Advent—Continue to learn new attitudes for prayer: while sitting quietly with palms open, breathe in the presence of God and exhale concerns and worries.

Christmas—While hurrying through the celebrations of Christmas, pause to record memories of Christmas in the air: breathe in and savor the seasonal smells outside, in the kitchen, around the tree.

Epiphany—Fill the season with fragrant offerings like the Magi's gift of frankincense: burn candles, light incense, display potpourri to create fragrant memories of God's presence.

SAVOR

Scripture: Psalm 34:8

Advent—During Advent preparations, offer to another the tastes from your own kitchen, or from your favorite bakery, and enjoy the sense of growth that comes from sharing.

Christmas—Invite someone to share the tastes of your Christmas table who otherwise might be alone.

Epiphany—Experiment with recipes for dishes from other cultures and celebrate Christ's birth for all the world.

FEEL

Scripture: Matthew 9:21

Advent—Offer to massage the shoulders of someone weary with the Christmas rush and welcome an exchange in kind!

Christmas—Hold hands with loved ones as you share Christmas memories.

Epiphany—Exchange handmade gifts from third world countries and bless the hands who crafted each item.

LOOK

Scripture: Luke 2:30

Advent—Prepare to see the meaning of Christmas more clearly this year by doing some devotional reading each day of Advent.

Christmas—Visit churches to view their manger scenes and to appreciate the lights and displays of the season.

Epiphany—Go out each evening to view the stars, remembering the star that guided the Magi to find Jesus, and ask God to guide your seeking.

O: OVERHEAD

PURPOSE

To make and use overhead projections in a traditional Christmas pageant, "What Do You See In The Manger?"

PREPARATION

- ❑ Acetate transparencies
- ❑ Fine-point permanent markers for transparencies
- ❑ Overhead projector
- ❑ Screen
- ❑ Bibles
- ❑ Manger
- ❑ Stool
- ❑ Costumes for Biblical characters
- ❑ Music for selected songs
- ❑ Accompaniment (optional)

PROCEDURE

"What Do You See In The Manger?" is a program design that offers a way to involve a wide variety of Sunday School classes and congregational members in the retelling of the traditional Christmas story. Using overhead projections prepared ahead of time by children ensures a unique interpretation of the meaning of God's gift of Christ in the manger. Such original artwork, however simple, generates interest and enthusiasm when children and parents anticipate their own illustrations as a part of the program.

To create this pageant, the following parts must be portrayed: Angel; Joseph; Mary; Narrator 1; Narrator 2; Shepherds; Wise Men.

Use simple costumes to enhance the experience. The only props required are a stool for Mary, a manger, an overhead projector, and a screen for the transparencies.

To make the overhead drawings, obtain a box of acetate transparencies and fine point permanent markers in a variety of colors. Determine the scenes to be projected during the narration, and assign different classes or students to design their interpretations of that part of the story. Suggested scenes include:

* the Prophets;
* Zechariah and Elizabeth;
* Simeon and Anna;
* Mary;
* Joseph;
* Mary and Angel;
* Mary and Joseph traveling;
* Bethlehem;
* Mary, Joseph, and Jesus in the stable;
* Shepherds in the field;
* Angel and Shepherds;
* Shepherds;
* Angel chorus;
* Shepherds at the manger;
* Kings traveling;
* Herod;
* Herod and Wise Men;
* Star;
* Wise Men at the manger;
* Manger;
* Personal interpretations.

Mark a script at the points where transparencies should be changed and vary the overhead projections as the narration unfolds for the first part of the program. Do NOT change transparencies during the character's dialogue with the narrator. Let the image of the manger remain the focus during these moments.

Musical selections are interspersed throughout the program and may be sung by Sunday School classes, soloists, small groups, or the congregation, or the carols may be played on a variety of instruments. Song suggestions include: "Angels We Have Heard On High," "Away In A Manger," "O Come, Little Children," "O Come, O Come Emmanuel," "Once In Royal David's City," "We Three Kings," "What Child Is This?"

At the end of the program, challenge the congregation to share their own view of the manger's gift. Depending upon the desires and comfort level of those gathered, several opportunities exist for the meaningful closing of this program. Original overhead drawings may be solicited ahead of time and narration written or given by the artist to explain the meaning of the illustration. Or, music and quiet reflection time may be offered instead. If desired, the final image of the manger may remain while people spontaneously or by prearrangement respond to the question "What do you see?" Regardless of the method selected, the program offers the opportunity for participants to decide for themselves what the gift of Christ means in each of their lives.

WHAT DO YOU SEE IN THE MANGER?

[If overhead transparencies are used during this section of the program, change the illustrations at appropriate points during the narration.]

Processional: "Once In Royal David's City"

THE PROPHECIES

Narrator 1: When we read the Old Testament prophecies we are astonished at the accurate details they give of the Savior's coming. A thousand years before Jesus was born, God selected the family of Jesse, father of King David, to prepare the way for the Messiah. Seven hundred years before Jesus was born Micah foretold the place of His birth. Isaiah, Jeremiah, Zechariah, and Malachi also made prophecies concerning the birth of Jesus.

Narrator 2: In New Testament times, too, there were many who prayed earnestly for the coming of the promised Redeemer. Among them were Zechariah and Elizabeth, the parents of John the Baptist, and the aged Simeon and Anna.

THE ANNUNCIATION

Narrator 1: There was a young woman named Mary who lived in Nazareth. She was engaged to marry a good man named Joseph, who was a carpenter. Both Mary and Joseph were descendants of King David. One day God sent the angel Gabriel to tell Mary that she had been chosen to be the mother of the Savior of the world. Soon the prophecies would be fulfilled.

Song: "O Come, O Come Emmanuel"

THE BIRTH OF JESUS

Narrator 2: *[As the narrator reads, Mary and Joseph proceed from the rear of the Church to the manger which is on the platform. Mary sits down on a stool at the far side of the manger while Joseph stands beside her looking into the manger.]* In those days a decree went out from Caesar Augustus that all the world should be enrolled. And Joseph also went up from Galilee, from the city of Nazareth, to Judea, to the city of David, which is called Bethlehem, because he was of the house and lineage of David, to be enrolled with Mary, his betrothed, who was with child.

Narrator 1: And while they were there, Mary gave birth to her first-born son and wrapped him in swaddling cloths, and laid him in a manger, because there was no place for them in the inn.

Song: "Away In A Manger"

THE STORY OF THE SHEPHERDS

Narrator 1: *[As the narrator speaks, the shepherds enter and stop midway of the platform.]* And in that region there were shepherds out in the field keeping watch over their flock by night. And an angel of the Lord appeared to them, and the glory of the Lord shone around them, and they were filled with fear. And the angel said to them:

Angel: *[Angel speaks from offstage or above congregation.]* Be not afraid; for behold, I bring you good news of a great joy which will come to all people; for to you is born this day in the city of David a Savior, who is Christ the Lord. And this will be a sign for you: you will find a babe wrapped in swaddling cloths and lying in a manger.

Narrator 2: The shepherds listened eagerly to the angel's words and when he finished they beheld a multitude of angels praising God and saying, "Glory to God in the highest, and on earth peace among those with whom he is well pleased."

Song: "Angels We Have Heard On High"

Narrator 1: *[While the Narrator continues, the Shepherds proceed to the platform and arrange themselves around the manger in a worshipful attitude.]* When the angels went away from them into heaven, the shepherds said to one another, "Let us go over to Bethlehem and see this thing that has happened, which the Lord has made known to us." And they went with haste, and found Mary and Joseph, and the babe lying in a manger.

Song: "O Come, Little Children"

THE STORY OF THE WISE MEN

Narrator 2: *[As the narrator reads, the Wise Men enter and proceed midway to the platform.]* Now when Jesus was born in Bethlehem of Judea in the days of Herod the king, behold, wise men from the East came to Jerusalem, saying, "Where is he who has been born King of the Jews? For we have seen his star in the east, and have come to worship him."

Narrator 1: When Herod the king heard this, he was troubled. They told him "In Bethlehem of Judea; for so it is written by the prophet." Then Herod summoned the wise men secretly and learned from them what time the star appeared; and sent them to Bethlehem, saying, "Go and search diligently for the child, and when you have found him bring me word, that I may come and worship him."

Narrator 2: *[As the Narrator continues, the Wise Men approach the platform and arrange themselves around the manger in a worshipful attitude.]* When the Wise Men left the king, the star which they had seen in the East led them southward. When they reached Bethlehem the star stood still over the stable where the manger was. As the Wise Men looked in that manger and saw

Baby Jesus, they knew that they had found the King about whom the prophets had written.

Narrator 1: And they fell down and worshiped him. Then, opening their treasures, they offered him gifts: gold and frankincense and myrrh.

Song: "We Three Kings"

WHAT THEY SAW IN THE MANGER

[If overhead transparencies are used, only project an illustration of the manger during this segment of the program.]

Narrator 2: Have you ever stopped to imagine what the people who saw Jesus in the manger that first Christmas night were thinking? Suppose we ask them.

Song: "What Child Is This?"

Narrator 1: What do you see, Joseph?

Joseph: What do I see in the manger? I see not my son, or Mary's child, but the Son of God — the fulfillment of the prophets words. "For to us a child is born, to us a son is given; and the government shall be upon his shoulders, and his name will be called Wonderful Counselor, Mighty God, Everlasting Father, Prince of Peace."

Narrator 2: Mary, what do you see in the manger?

Mary: My soul magnifies the Lord, and my spirit rejoices in God, my Savior, for He who is mighty has done great things for me, and holy is His name. I see in the babe the Christ. That is what Gabriel announced to me. That is what the angels sang. These promises I ponder in my heart.

Narrator 1: Angel, you who hovered with others of the heavenly host over the fields of Bethlehem, and who spoke to the shepherds, what do you see in the manger?

Angel: I see the Savior. I declare to one and all, "To you is born this day a Savior, who is Christ the Lord."

Narrator 2: What do you see, Shepherd?

Shepherd: I see the angel's promise fulfilled. They told us of peace on earth to people of good will. That is what I see in the manger — a child who shall be the Prince of Peace and who shall bring peace to this restless earth.

Narrator 1: You Wise Men who followed the star till it rested over the manger. What do you see in the manger to repay your long journey from the far East?

Wise Men: We asked Herod where the newborn King of the Jews could be found. Then the star by which God guided us led us to this humble manger. But here we see, not only the King of the

Jews, but the King of Love who commands the allegiance of every heart; the Savior God gave to the world.

Song: "What Child Is This?" - Chorus

Narrator 1 *[To congregation]*: What do YOU see in the manger? *[Responses may include a moment of meditation, an instrumental selection, overhead drawings, pre-planned answers or spontaneous personal testimonies.]*

Benediction: Away In A Manger - Verse 3
Be near me, Lord Jesus;
I ask Thee to stay
Close by me forever,
and love me, I pray.
Bless all the dear children
In Thy tender care.
Prepare us for Heaven, to live with Thee there.

P: PUPPETS

PURPOSE

To make and use giant puppets to tell the Christmas story.

PREPARATION

- ❏ Plastic garbage bags, large
- ❏ Newspaper
- ❏ Cardboard poles
- ❏ Duct tape
- ❏ Masking tape
- ❏ Construction paper
- ❏ Scissors
- ❏ Glue
- ❏ Paper tablecloth, fabric or crepe paper
- ❏ Yarn, fake fur or fiberfil
- ❏ Paper plates

PROCEDURE

What do plastic bottles, paper bags, aluminum cans, cardboard egg cartons, and daily newspapers have in common? They are all throw-away objects, recyclable items, environmental concerns, and puppet materials. But what do these things have to do with Advent prophecies, Christmas stories, and Epiphany themes? A lot! Use puppets in worship as the children's message, the characters in a program or pageant, or the sermon; in education for making announcements, leading singing, and telling stories; in nurture for intergenerational activities, potluck suppers and talent shows; in Outreach for community events, nursing home visits, and work camps.

Ideas and instructions are provided for "giant" puppets to use during the Christmas season.

Form giant puppets from throw-away materials. The puppets will be easier to make if several people or teams work on the project.

Construct the head of the puppet from a large plastic garbage bag. To make it stronger, use several bags inside of each other. Hold open the bags.

Unfold the newspaper and stack it on a pile. Crumple the newspaper, one sheet at a time, and stuff it into the open bag. It is important to crumple it one sheet at a time or the puppet head will become too lumpy. Be sure the weight is distributed as evenly as possible. When the bag is approximately half full, insert the pole into the middle of the newspaper. Continue stuffing the bag. When the bag is full, gather the top of it around the pole and tape it securely. Turn the puppet upside down. Continue to hold the puppet while the features and costume are added.

Make rolls of duct tape to use to stick the features to the puppet. Cut two eyes from construction paper or paper plates and attach them to the face. Cut a nose, ears and a mouth and affix them to the head.

Make hair from yarn, fibrefil or another material and attach it to the top of the stuffed bag.

Construct a simple costume from packaging material, paper tablecloth, bags, or lightweight fabric, such as an old sheet. Snip a hole in the center of the piece, and slide it up the pole. Tape it into place around the neck of the puppet. Trim with additional scraps to create the desired effect.

Use the tube to carry and operate the puppet.

 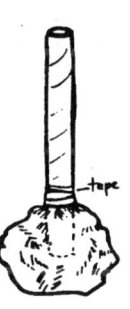 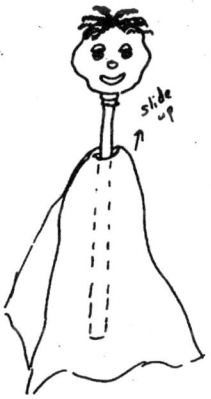

Q: QUESTIONS

PURPOSE

To use critical thinking skills to examine the reasons behind specific Christmas customs and family traditions.

PREPARATION

- ❑ Paper
- ❑ Pencils or pens
- ❑ Bible
- ❑ Objects related to Christmas traditions (optional)

PROCEDURE

Often traditions become so ingrained that families "go through the motions" of the holidays without stopping to think about reasons behind seasonal celebrations. Critical thinking challenges the brain to examine, analyze, see relationships and patterns, and form opinions regarding ideas and subjects. At the heart of critical thinking skills lies the ability to ask open-ended questions, to consider "why" something is, to ask questions that can't be answered by "yes" or "no" or other one-word responses.

The Jewish religion understood the need to encourage examination of customs and traditions. The celebration of Passover, for example, would not be complete without the asking of the "four questions" that require the older generation to explain the reasons behind the ritual of the seder meal to the youngest people present. Since Christmas is the celebration of the arrival of a baby to His Jewish parents, perhaps it would be appropriate to adopt this Jewish custom of asking questions in order to celebrate His birth.

Determine a moment in your family's or church family's Christmas traditions when it would be appropriate to take time to ask and answer some critical questions that reveal the reasons for all the special foods, gifts, decorations, or rituals. Develop four open-ended questions that permit the explanation of your most cherished Christmas traditions. Some examples might include the following:

QUESTION ONE

On other days, we go to church in the morning. Why on this night do we go to church so late?

RESPONSE: On Christmas Eve, we remember that it was at night as the shepherds watched their sheep that the angels came to announce the birth of a special baby. The shepherds heard the angel chorus because they were awake and watching. On Christmas Eve, we want to be awake and watching for the birth of Jesus, too. So we share a special service with our friends at church to remember that Jesus, the Prince of Peace, was born in the gentle quiet of the night.

QUESTION TWO

When it is someone's birthday, we usually bring presents to the birthday girl or boy. Why on Jesus' birthday do we give presents to one another?

RESPONSE: On Jesus' birthday we give presents because the Wise Men brought gifts of gold, frankincense, and myrrh to the baby Jesus. Jesus also taught us that the way to show our love for Him was to love one another. So on Christmas we share gifts, like the Wise Men did, but we share them with others in Jesus' name.

QUESTION THREE

For no other holiday do we put up a tree inside the house. Why for this holiday do we bring a tree inside and put lights on it?

RESPONSE: Many years ago in Germany, the tradition of using a lighted tree at Christmas was begun. The green boughs of the evergreen tree symbolize for us that the gift Jesus brings is eternal life. The twinkling lights remind us that Jesus is the Light of the World. The beauty of the lighted Christmas tree suggests the beauty of God's love for the world, a love that sent Jesus, God's only Son.

QUESTION FOUR

At no other time do we set up a nativity scene. Why only at Christmas do we worship the baby in the manger?

RESPONSE: We worship God Almighty, the Maker of the Universe. Yet our human bodies cannot see or understand the power that God is. Because God wanted us to know how much we are loved, Jesus came as a baby, a human, just like us. The nativity scene reminds us of how God's love came to earth, love made known in Jesus, our Savior.

Adapt these questions to your own needs, or create others that reflect special ethnic or cultural traditions that the younger generation needs to come to understand (and of which older ones need to be reminded). Young readers could read the questions, non-readers would need to be prompted. While reading the answers is possible, sharing the reasons in your own words is more meaningful.

R: RIBBONS

PURPOSE

To construct ribbon banners to convey the theme of Christmas worship services.

PREPARATION

- ❏ Altar cloth; white, green, purple or dark blue
- ❏ Ribbon, 4 to 6 inches wide and as long as needed to fit across the top of a table and to hang over the front.
- ❏ Scissors
- ❏ Velcro dots
- ❏ Letters or letter stencils
- ❏ Fabric paints
- ❏ Brushes
- ❏ Iron
- ❏ Candles (appropriate colors for Advent and Christmas)
- ❏ Candle holders
- ❏ Duct tape
- ❏ Pins

PROCEDURE

In keeping with a seasonal theme, decorate the altar or worship table with a ribbon and candle for each week preceding Christmas.

Cover the worship area with a purple or dark blue cloth, depending on the congregation's tradition. Measure six white ribbons long enough to reach across the table and to hang down in front of the altar.

Letter words vertically on the ribbons, for example: HOPE, PEACE, FAITH, LOVE, JOY and LIFE, or any words that correspond with the seasonal theme. Purchase ready-made letters to glue or iron on. Another method for lettering is to use stencils and fabric paint. Letters should be large, easy to read and in black, purple or dark blue. Be sure that the words are on the portion of the ribbon that hangs over the front of the altar table.

Fasten Velcro dots to the top end of the ribbon and to the back of the altar cloth; use duct tape circles or pins to prevent ribbons from shifting. Add ribbons from left to right; place a candle on each ribbon along the top of the table. The candles will be lighted each week as a new candle is added. Place the Christ Candle in the center of the arrangement; light it on Christmas Eve or Christmas Day.

The altar cloth can be changed to white for Christmas and green for Epiphany. Another option for the worship table would be to use a white cloth throughout this holy season and to change the ribbon colors. Experiment with shiny gold letters for a more festive look; be sure they are legible from a distance.

To create a banner, follow instructions for lettering ribbons with words to convey the theme. Instead of arranging the ribbons on the table, fasten them to a dowel or brass cafe curtain rod. Ribbons may be attached to a rectangle of fabric which corresponds with the altar cloth or the strips may move freely without a background. Matching the banner to the altar will help to co-ordinate the church's Advent, Christmas and Epiphany worship environment.

Reinforce the theme for the season by making individual ribbon banners at an Advent workshop or in Sunday School classes. Use the same methods, but on a smaller scale. Choose floral, craft or gift-wrap ribbon; use smaller stencils or self-stick letters and small dowels. Add gold cord to form a hanger.

S: SENSES

PURPOSE

To use sight, smell, sound, taste and touch related learning activities to explore Christmas themes.

PREPARATION

❑ Supplies vary with project.

PROCEDURE

The twelve days of Christmas bombard the senses with much to see, hear, smell, taste, and touch. But rather than feeling overwhelmed, participants who have been prepared throughout Advent can be ready to connect Christmas impressions with the sustaining message of faith and share it throughout Epiphany and the new year. Explore the Christmas message through the five senses by using any or all of these learning activities in Sunday School classes, Mid-week ministries, Family nights, and youth groups.

SIGHT

ACTIVITY

Stained glass window ornaments

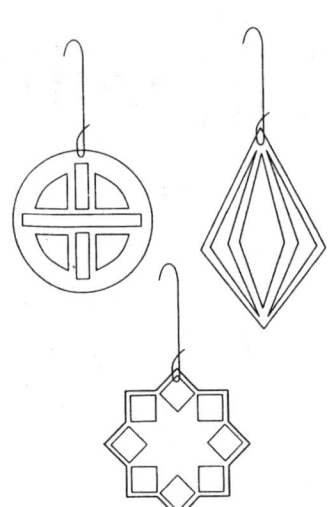

MATERIALS

- Black paper
- Waxed paper
- Crepe paper in primary and secondary colors
- Scissors
- Glue sticks

72

- Tape
- Cord

METHOD

Beautiful sights to see at Christmas time include illustrations of jewel-toned stained glass windows. The brilliant images appear on greeting cards, gift wrap, and decorations. Take time to enjoy any stained glass windows in churches.

Make a simple ornament as a keepsake. Cut 9" x 12" paper into fourths, then fold the smaller rectangles in half to cut symmetrical ornament shapes. While the paper is folded, cut openings along the fold line. Carefully poke a scissor point into the paper to cut additional openings on each side of the fold line. The more openings there are, the more colorful the ornament will be.

Cut crepe paper pieces larger than each opening and glue them onto the back with a glue stick. Tape waxed paper behind the glued crepe paper to help hold shapes in place. Attach cord loops to hang the ornaments.

The crepe paper colors look dull until they are placed near a light source. Hang the decorations in a window and see the jewel-like colors appear.

SMELL

ACTIVITY

Pomander Balls

MATERIALS

- Firm oranges
- Whole cloves
- Cinnamon
- Orris root (look in spice aisle at grocery, drug or herb stores)
- Glue
- Awls or skewers
- Plastic bags

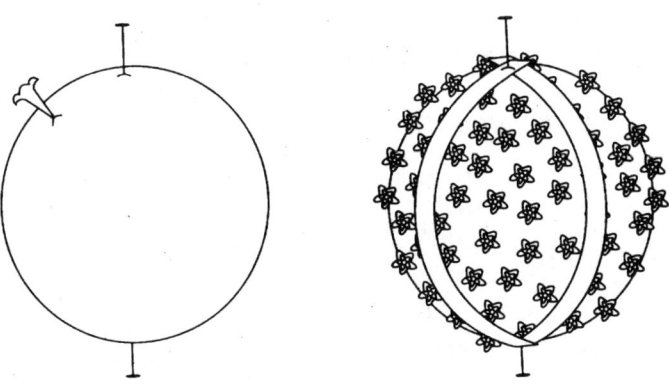

- Cheesecloth
- Scissors
- Ribbon
- Cord
- Straight pins

METHOD

The aromatic combination of citrus and spice is a traditional scent of Christmas in potpourri, teas, baked goods and seasoning. Pomander balls made from oranges and cloves make a fragrant and useful gift. For hundreds of years homemakers have used them to freshen the air, to fight illnesses, and to discourage moths.

To make one pomander ball, you will need one firm orange; 2 to 3 ounces of whole cloves; one tablespoon of ground cinnamon and 2 teaspoons of ground orris root. If orris root is omitted, add more cinnamon or 1/2 teaspoon of allspice.

Use an awl or skewer to punch holes in the orange skin. A random pattern works best; too many holes in a straight line might cause a split in the skin. Insert whole cloves into the pre-punched pattern covering most of the surface of the orange.

Mix the ground spices in a plastic bag, then place the fruit into the bag and twist the top to close it. Gently shake the clove-studded orange to coat it with the other spices.

Tie the pomander into a square of cheesecloth allowing air to circulate around it. Hang it in a cool, dry place so the orange will shrink and become hard. This takes about three weeks.

Remove the cheesecloth and give the pomander its finishing touches. Tie a ribbon around the orange and knot it; tie a second ribbon crossing over the first ribbon at the bottom and knot at the top. Push straight pins in at the bottom and top to secure criss-crossed ribbons. Attach a cord for hanging. Glue on a bow or dried flowers for a more decorative pomander. Enjoy the scent for many weeks after Christmas.

SOUND

ACTIVITY

Mini Jingle Bell Wreaths

MATERIALS

- Ruffled fabric ponytail holders in dark or bright green
- Jingle bells
- Red or plaid ribbon
- Needles

- Green thread
- Scissors

METHOD

One of the favorite sounds of Christmas is the happy music of jingle bells. We might hear tiny tinkling bells attached to holiday jewelry and decor or the resonant ringing of sleigh bells.

Here is a jingle bell wreath to wear or to put on a doorknob to add music to the whole "symphony of Christmas"!

Sew jingle bells all over the ponytail holder. Arrange them in clusters or scatter them all around the fabric. Sew the bells in place using heavy or double thread. Add large or small bows by tacking them to the fabric.

Stretch the ruffle-covered elastic to fit around a doorknob, to encircle the wrist, or to dress up a ponytail. The jingle bell wreath will become part of the sounds of the season.

TASTE

ACTIVITY

Gingerbread With Toppings

MATERIALS

- Ingredients in recipes
- Equipment and utensils
- Work surface
- Oven
- Foil pans (8" x 8")
- Foil to cover finished dessert

METHOD

A familiar taste of Christmas is gingerbread. This favorite dessert may appear as a cookie, cake or Gingerbread house. Try gingerbread in a different form; start a new family tradition!

Check cookbooks to find recipes for cookies, cakes and breads flavored with ginger and other spices.

Follow recipe directions. For a quick and tasty pan of gingerbread, try one of the mixes from the supermarket. Add a festive touch by offering one of these toppings.

RECIPE FOR LEMON SAUCE

* 1/2 c. sugar
* 1 tablespoon cornstarch
* 1/4 teaspoon salt
* 1/4 cup cold water
* 3/4 cup boiling water

* 3 tablespoons fresh lemon juice
* 1 teaspoon grated lemon rind
* 1/2 teaspoon vanilla extract
* 2 tablespoons butter

Combine sugar, cornstarch and salt. Mix in cold water. Gradually stir in boiling water and cook for 3 minutes or until smooth, clear and slightly thickened. Add remaining ingredients. Makes about 1 1/2 cups. Serve warm or cold.

RECIPE FOR CREAM CHEESE TOPPING

* 3 ounce package cream cheese
* 1 tablespoon sugar
* 3 tablespoons milk
* 1 teaspoon grated lemon rind
* Few drops lemon juice
* Ground nuts (optional)

Cream all ingredients together. Spoon over gingerbread. Sprinkle with nuts. Makes about 1/2 cup.

Brew a pot of tea and savor the spicy gingerbread. Share!

TOUCH

ACTIVITY

Evergreen Prints

MATERIALS

- Evergreen branches
- Newspaper
- Heavy books
- Brushes
- Paint (fabric paint for sweatshirts or other cloth projects)
- Pencils
- Scrap paper
- Paper or cloth items
- Clean up supplies

METHOD

The Christmas setting would not seem complete without the varied textures and distinctive fragrance of evergreens.

Have you ever touched different types of evergreen branches? Some feel prickly and some feel silky. Gather small cuttings from your Christmas tree or from evergreens in the yard. Blue spruce, cedar, yew or juniper will work well for this texture painting project.

Decide what your finished project will be: note paper, greeting cards, wrapping paper, place mats, apron or sweatshirt. Cut and fold heavy white paper for notes and greeting cards. To make wrapping paper, separate sheets of tissue paper and place over newspaper before printing. For printing on sweatshirts or other cloth articles, follow directions on fabric paint containers. Choose evergreen boughs that are small enough to print on the paper or fabric you have prepared. Evergreens that are less bulky and are a little flatter will produce a clear print. Flatten branches between several sheets of newspaper which are weighted down with heavy books or irons.

Experiment on scrap paper to find the right color and the correct amount of paint. Brush paint on one side of the evergreen branch; firmly press onto the paper or fabric. After printing, lift the branch carefully to prevent the lines from smudging.

Make fingerprint dots for berries or paint tiny pine cones for added interest. Allow the paint to dry. Enjoy the textured evergreen prints and make extras to give as gifts.

T: TABLEAU

PURPOSE

To design a series of still-life dramas, called tableaus, to illustrate Christmas carols.

PREPARATION

- ❑ Music for selected carols
- ❑ Accompaniment (optional)
- ❑ Costumes
- ❑ Props

PROCEDURE

Design a "Living Christmas Carols" presentation as an all-church program or as a special service during the holiday season. Stage it as simply or as elaborately as time, space, and talent seem to dictate. For a special event, set different scenes at reasonable distances for visitors to walk past or use different rooms in the building, each for a different carol. For worship or a more formal pageant, stage one scene after another in the same location, such as a sanctuary or social hall. If scenes are set one at a time, consider creating a "frame" for a stage — perhaps even in the shape of a hymn book. Draw a curtain or turn out lights while each carol is re-set and transformed into a living picture. Use additional spot lighting, if possible. Add costumes to enhance the presentation.

Use choir members or congregational singing to provide carols in the background of the still-life scenes — called tableaus — staged for a worship service or program. For other special events, have a choir member guide a small group to view the tableaus and lead the group in singing the carols. If vocal talent is lacking, use instruments or pre-recorded music to accompany each setting. The number of people in each scene, or the number of carols portrayed, may depend upon available participants.

LIVING CHRISTMAS CAROL SUGGESTIONS

FIRST PICTURE: "O Come All Ye Faithful"

For a modern portrayal, set a scene with several children or adults kneeling in prayer. One stands in the midst of the group with an open Bible. Or use a more traditional interpretation of a Christmas scene with shepherds kneeling at a manger.

SECOND PICTURE: "While Shepherds Watched Their Flocks"

One shepherd points to the sky, two face the ground as though frightened, and one kneels in prayer. If more shepherds are used in the scene they may stand with crooks or staffs in hand.

THIRD PICTURE: "Hark the Herald Angels"

Shepherds stand in an attitude of wonder, listening intently to sounds from above. Vary positions and levels to create an interesting tableau.

FOURTH PICTURE: "It Came Upon the Midnight Clear"

Many angels on levels surrounded by cotton batting or angel hair to suggest clouds. Group in twos and threes, with one or two separate angels reclining on their sides as though resting in the heavens and looking toward the earth. "Harps of gold," if possible, add a nice touch.

FIFTH PICTURE: "Away In A Manger"

Mary seated in attitude of prayerful devotion beside a rude manger bed containing a baby or doll. Joseph stands behind Mary.

SIXTH PICTURE: "We Three Kings"

Three boys or men representing the three kings stand together, each with a special gift for the Christ child. One might be consulting a scroll with constellations drawn, another gazing ahead into the heavens, and the other in an attitude of prayer.

SEVENTH PICTURE: "Silent Night"

Mary sits near the manger bed. Joseph stands at her side. Shepherds are positioned at left in prayerful attitude. Wise men kneel at right with gifts extended toward manger. Angels in background.

U: USE

PURPOSE

To experience Christmas music through the five senses.

PREPARATION

❑ Supplies vary with project.

PROCEDURE

Singing carols is one thing; sensing them is another! Use a variety of activities to accentuate the sights, smells, sounds, tastes, and touches associated with the words and music of the songs of Christmas. Use the ideas in Sunday School classes, youth group meetings, Junior and Senior High retreats, service projects, and other special events.

SIGHT

- Capture the concept contained in the carol by photographing modern day scenes related to it.
- Construct mobiles that depict hymn stories.
- Draw scenes from various carols on acetate transparencies and display them on an overhead projector.
- View paintings from various periods of art and match one with each carol.

SMELL

- Develop a game listing ten carols on the left side of the paper and ten smells on the right side of the sheet. Match the answers.
- Prepare bags with scents suggested in carols and guess the smells associated with the songs.
- Purchase scratch 'n sniff stickers and match one with each carol.
- Write a guided meditation based on the words of a carol and incorporate various smells into the script.

SOUND

- Attend a concert and listen to the music of the season.
- Challenge participants to "Name That Tune".
- Read the story of a carol before or after singing it.
- Simulate sound effects to match the lyrics.

TASTE

- Bake bread and remember that Bethlehem means "city of bread".
- Get a taste of various types of music by playing recordings of carols performed by various groups.
- Match a different feeling or mood with each carol and journal about a taste of love, joy, peace, and so forth.
- Taste foods from the country where the carol originated, or from the period of history to which it refers.

TOUCH

- Arrange an assortment of objects, create a worship center, and encourage people to touch the display!
- Create a collage — small or large, individual or group.
- Form a three-dimensional bulletin board related to one or more carols.
- Make books about a carol and put a different texture on each page. Give the completed projects to young children or to people with impaired vision.

V: VISUALS

PURPOSE

To proclaim the Christmas story in visual ways.

PREPARATION

❏ Supplies vary with project.

PROCEDURE

The Christian community is challenged to reclaim Christmas as the celebration of the Savior's birth. Churches must take responsibility for "broadcasting" the story of Christmas in as many ways as possible.

The holiday season is rich with visual symbols and many types of displays. Most of the displays relate to the secular or commercial aspects of the season. Since municipal religious displays are not allowed in some communities, churches and individual families must make a greater effort to portray the Christmas story.

Congregations have traditionally made use of lawn displays, outdoor signs and seasonal newspaper messages to visualize the true meaning of Christmas. Add something new! Brainstorm with a Christmas task force to find creative new "sights" that reach out to the community. Begin new traditions which are a "feast for the eyes" and declare the birth of Christ.

BANNERS AND FLAGS

Colorful, weather-resistant banners and flags have appeared in neighborhoods everywhere. Create banners or flags with religious symbols to highlight the season. Arrange a family workshop where participants can share patterns and instructions as they work together to create a banner or flag to display at home. Or, construct a series of banners to surround church property.

ETHNIC ENHANCEMENTS

Research and enjoy customs from other countries. Which ethnic groups are represented in your congregation and community? Many traditions from other cultures will add richly to the visual aspect of the holiday season: parades, Posadas, luminaries and costumes.

LIFE-SIZE DISPLAY FIGURES

Check for large nativity scene patterns in craft books, woodworking supply stores, hardware stores, and libraries. Follow directions for weather-proofing and stabilizing figures. This will provide an opportunity for members with woodworking and painting skills to share their talents.

LIVE NATIVITY

Arrange for a living tableau to be viewed for several evenings. Add interest by using farm animals. Check with a local zoo to see if they will allow a live nativity as part of their winter programming.

Consider special geographical characteristics. Sculpt snow and ice in a frosty climate or shape sand figures at the beach! Create a rustic manger scene in a rural setting or a cave creche in a hilly or mountainous region.

WINDOW MURALS

Buildings with large windows are ideal for mural painting. Enlist the help of skilled people who can outline the scene and direct the painting process. Organize the youth or other groups to fill in the drawing. Check with a paint supply store or art shop for the best paints to use on windows.

W: WISE MEN

PURPOSE

To dramatize the story of the Wise Men.

PREPARATION

❏ Costumes (optional)

PROCEDURE

Present the story of the Magi, Matthew 2:1-12, in a dramatic way. Characters needed include a Narrator, Herod, King One, King Two, King Three, and Chief Priests. To involve more people, create acting "groups" to represent the kings and chief priests.

Presentation will vary based on skills, preparation time, and performance needs. In Sunday School classes or worship services, a simple choral reading may be done with stools for actors and music stands to hold scripts, or readers may be scattered throughout the congregation and speak from the pews. A more elaborate production with costumes and memorized parts would make a meaningful seasonal program or devotion.

No matter the level of presentation, participants should be encouraged to practice the script aloud several times and to rehearse when to stand and speak. Readers should be reminded to breathe deeply and project voices, to read with feeling, slowly and distinctly.

SCRIPT

NARRATOR *[Facing congregation]*: Now, when Jesus was born in Bethlehem of Judea in the days of Herod the King [Herod stands, smiles, and gestures in a "kingly" way] behold, wise men from the East came to Jerusalem [three kings or teams stand] saying,

KING 1: Where is he who has been born king of the Jews?

KING 2: For we have seen his star in the East,

KING 3: And have come to worship him. *[Bow from the waist.]*

NARRATOR: When Herod the king heard this, he was troubled *[Herod stands, growls and complains]* and all Jerusalem with him *[Priests growl and complain]*. And assembling all the chief priests and scribes of the people *[Priests stand]* he inquired of them:

HEROD: Where is the Christ supposed to be born?

CHIEF PRIESTS: In Bethlehem of Judea; for so it is written by the prophet:

ONE PROPHETIC CHIEF PRIEST: "And you, O Bethlehem, in the land of Judah, are by no means least among the rulers of Judah; for from you shall come a ruler who will govern my people Israel."

NARRATOR: Then Herod summoned the Wise Men secretly and ascertained from them what time the star appeared *[Herod gestures and Wise Men turn toward Herod]*; and he sent them to Bethlehem, saying:

HEROD: *[Insincerely]* Go and search diligently for the child, and when you have found him bring me word, that I too may come and worship him. *[Wise Men bow and nod agreement.]*

NARRATOR: When they had heard the king they went their way. *[Herod and priest sit.]*

KINGS: Let's go! Follow that star! There it goes!

NARRATOR: And lo, the star which they had seen in the East went before them, till it came to rest over the place where the child was.

A KING: In that stable???

NARRATOR: When they saw the star they rejoiced exceedingly!

KINGS: *[Quietly]* Yay!

NARRATOR: And going into the house they saw the child with Mary his mother, and they fell down and worshiped him. *[Kings bow, or kneel, and look worshipful.]* Then, opening their treasures, they offered him gifts.

KING 1: Gold!

KING 2: Frankincense!

KING 3: And myrrh!

NARRATOR: And being warned in a dream not to return to Herod *[The kings make a "sh-h-h-h!" sign and pretend to tiptoe away as Herod stands]*, they departed to their own country by another way *[Kings sit as Herod looks around, then shrugs and sits.]* And so ends our lesson of the visit of the Magi. Let those who are wise still listen to the angel's voices and follow the light of the Bethlehem star! *[Narrator sits.]*

X: X-CHANGE

PURPOSE

To "(e)x-change" Christmas gifts that "(e)x-press" the true meaning of the season.

PREPARATION

- ❏ Shoe boxes
- ❏ Wrapping paper
- ❏ Construction paper
- ❏ Scissors
- ❏ Tape
- ❏ Bows
- ❏ Markers

PROCEDURE

At Christmas, God gave His Son, Jesus, to be the Savior of the world. In response to this great gift, people continue to give and receive presents as signs of love for God and for others. This activity involves gifts which cost little or no money. Give them to family, friends, neighbors, and others as expressions of gratitude to God.

Cover the lid and the bottom of the box with Christmas paper. Wrap the two pieces separately. Place a bow on the cover. Cut twenty-five strips of construction or wrapping paper and write one "Gift" on each piece. Choose from the suggestions provided, or brainstorm additional ideas. Place the strips in the box and put the cover on it. Choose a strip and give a "gift" each day for twenty-five days.

GIFT SUGGESTIONS

- Help prepare a family meal.
- Visit a long lived person.
- Write a letter to a loved one.
- Shovel or sweep the sidewalk of a neighbor.

- Invite a friend for cocoa and conversation.
- Go caroling in the neighborhood.
- Bake cookies and give a dozen away.
- Babysit for someone with a small child.
- Read the Christmas story to a person with poor sight.
- Write Christmas cards to or for shut-ins.
- Take a person shopping who doesn't drive.
- Eat simply and give the extra money to a charity.
- Bake bread and give a loaf away.
- Volunteer in a soup kitchen.
- Make Christmas ornaments that can be given away.
- Deliver food baskets to those in need.
- Share gently used toys with community agencies.
- Bring a small decorated tree to someone who doesn't have one.
- Make favors to be used on hospital trays.
- Have a family cleaning day and cooperate together to prepare for the Christmas "Guest".
- Share a smile and friendly word with a sales clerk.
- Pray for each member of the family.
- Invite neighborhood children over to play games.
- Become a pen pal with someone in another country.
- Volunteer time at a local food bank.

Y: YOUTH

PURPOSE

To involve youth in Christmas service projects for people of all ages.

PREPARATION

❑ Supplies vary with project.

PROCEDURE

Youth groups can use the season of Christmas as a time to learn how to give to people of all ages. Allow the youth to choose a few possibilities for ministry from the age-appropriate list below, or to create their own plan for reaching out to others during the holidays.

PRE-SCHOOL

- Provide a baby sitting service, either in-home or at church, for parents to do Christmas shopping.
- Make quilts for hospitalized children or cradle roll infants.
- Do a pre-school "story hour" at the church or at a library on a Christmas theme.

LOWER ELEMENTARY

- Offer affordable gifts for children to purchase for family members, guide their shopping, and help them wrap and label presents.
- Take a group of children caroling to a mall, zoo, or nursing home.
- Provide a "cabin fever" party during winter break from school with videos, games, and refreshments.

UPPER ELEMENTARY

- Help youth design their own cards and wrapping paper for family gifts.
- Involve upper elementary young people in creating a Christmas basket for a needy family.

- Visit shut-ins with hand-made gifts, and help them decorate for Christmas.

MIDDLE SCHOOL

- Hold a bowling party and raise money for a charitable cause with pledges for pins.
- Take a group to shovel walks or do outside clean up for shut-ins.
- Organize a scavenger hunt for simple gifts like bars of soap and toothpaste to give to mental health organizations.

HIGH SCHOOL

- Invite a friend to youth activities at church.
- Sponsor a Christmas party for area youth groups.
- Collect food for a community pantry or animal shelter.

ADULT

- Offer a free gift-wrapping service.
- Help with Christmas decorating and baking for families in the congregation and community.
- Hang outside lights for those who can't or are too busy.

OLDER ADULT

- Address Christmas cards and help write notes.
- Read the Christmas story for someone whose eyes are dim.
- Share a meal rather than just dropping it off.

Z: Z-A PEOPLE

PURPOSE

To teach the Christmas story through a variety of methods.

PREPARATION

❑ Supplies vary with project.

PROCEDURE

The story of Christmas unfolds with a large cast of characters. Take a piece of paper and make a list from A to Z of all the names you can think of related to the story told during this season of the church year. The list might include A - Angels, B - Baby Jesus, C - Caesar, D - David, E - Elizabeth, F - Father Joseph, G - Gabriel, H - Herod, I - Innkeeper, J - John the Baptist, K - Keepers of sheep, L - Leaders, M - Mary, N - Nameless people, O - Old Anna, P - Prophets, Q - Quirinius, R - Roman soldiers, S - Simeon, T - Travelers on the road, U - Upset people, V - Villagers of Bethlehem, W - Wise Men, X - Xtras, Y - Youth, Z - Zechariah.

Teach the stories of these, and other, people through a variety of methods.

ARCHITECTURE

- Visit churches named after people whose stories we tell during Christmas; Consider making a photo collage of the sites.
- Create a scavenger hunt to find Christmas symbols or people represented in stained glass windows.

ART

- Make masks to represent the faces of people and use them to help tell the story of this season.
- Build a table-top model depicting one of the scenes of Christ's birth.

BANNERS/TEXTILES

- Design a banner for each week representing a person and his or her story.
- Sew a costume and represent one of the characters highlighted during this season.

CREATIVE WRITING

- Write a comparison showing the similarities between the crowds in Bethlehem long ago and the crowds in the malls today.
- Write a description of events from the point of view of one of the people in the Christmas story.

CULINARY

- Bake cookies in the shapes of some of the symbols of Christmas.
- Hold an all church supper featuring Christmas breads from around the world.

DANCE/MOVEMENT

- Add gestural interpretation to a favorite Christmas carol.
- Perform "Joy To The World" and involve worshipers in movement.

DRAMA

- Perform a first-person monologue of one of the people from the stories of the season.
- Create a tableau to depict events of Christmas.

GAMES

- Devise "Bingo" cards with the names of people in the Christmas story.
- Choose a favorite game format (Concentration, Go Fish, or Password) and adapt it to teach the names of the people of Christmas.

MUSIC

- Use familiar tunes to make up songs about people in the stories.
- Perform a Christmas musical celebrating the life of Jesus.

PHOTOGRAPHY

- Take photos (or cut photos from magazines) to match faces with descriptions of the characters of the Christmas story.
- Make a 25 day calendar with pictures of people who represent the faces of Christmas.

PUPPETRY

- Make finger puppets and tell a story to a small group.
- Draw a figure of a person on a piece of cardboard or posterboard; Cut out holes for the head and the arms and "get into" the picture.

STORYTELLING

- Retell a Christmas story from the Bible using a "round robin" approach, with each person adding 3 to 5 words to complete the plot.
- Associate an object with each person and tell a story from that object's point of view, like the frankincense from a Wise Man.

RESOURCES

Berglund, Mary Catherine. <u>Gather The Children - Cycle A</u>. Washington, DC: The Pastoral Press, 1989.

——-. <u>Gather The Children - Cycle B</u>. Washington, DC: The Pastoral Press, 1987.

——-. <u>Gather The Children - Cycle C</u>. Washington, DC: The Pastoral Press, 1987.

Brown, Carolyn C. <u>Gateways To Worship - A Year Of Worship Experiences For Young Children</u>. Nashville: Abingdon, 1989.

Cronin, Gaynell Bordes. <u>Holy Days & Holidays - Prayer Celebrations with Children</u>. Minneapolis: Winston Press, 1979, 1985.

Editors. <u>Children's Church for 2's and 3's--Leader's Guide.</u> Elgin, IL: David C. Cook, 1991.

Editors. <u>Great Worship for Kids.</u> Cincinnati, OH: Standard Publishing, 1992.

Fogle, Jeanne S. and Bea Weidner, Illustrator. <u>Seasons of God's Love - The Church Year</u>. Philadelphia: The Geneva Press, 1988.

Hickman, Hoyt L., Don E. Saliers, Laurence Hull Stookey, and James F. White. <u>Handbook of the Christian Year</u>. Nashville: Abingdon, 1986, 1990.

Hillard, Dick and George Collopy, Illustrator. <u>The Lord Blesses Me</u>. Saratoga, CA: Resource Publications, 1978.

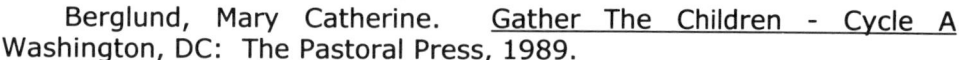, Catherine A. <u>Through The Christian Year</u>. Nashville: Abingdon, 1983.

——-. <u>A Rainbow Of Seasons</u>. Minneapolis: Augsburg, 1983.

Mathson, Patricia. <u>Pray & Play</u>. Notre Dame, IN: Ave Maria Press, 1989.

Rezy, Carol. <u>Liturgies For Little Ones</u>. Notre Dame, IN: Ave Maria Press, 1978.

Rock, Louise H., Editor. <u>Children's Church For Kindergartners — Year 2</u>. Elgin, IL: David C. Cook, 1975.

Smith, Judy Gattis. <u>Birth, Death, And Resurrection — Teaching Spiritual Growth Through the Church Year</u>. Nashville: Abingdon, 1989.
——-. <u>Celebrating Special Days In The Church School Year</u>. Colorado Springs, CO: Meriwether Publishing Ltd., 1981.

Stadler, Bernice. <u>Celebrations Of The Word For Children — Cycle A</u>. Mystic, CT: Twenty-Third Publications, 1989.
——-. <u>Celebrations Of The Word For Children — Cycle B</u>. Mystic, CT: Twenty-Third Publications, 1987.
——-. <u>Celebrations Of The Word For Children — Cycle C</u>. Mystic, CT: Twenty-Third Publications, 1988.

Willmington, H. L. <u>Willmington's Book of Bible Lists</u>. Wheaton, IL: Tyndale, 1987.
Wilson, Jan and Linda Herd, Illustrator. <u>Feasting For Festivals</u>. Batavia, IL: Lion, 1990.

Also:

Numerous Bible story books and commentaries.